Vicky Whipple

Lesbian Widows
Invisible Grief

Pre-publication
REVIEW . . .

"**I**n her careful examination of the grief that dare not speak its name, Dr. Whipple does a wonderful job of bringing the silent suffering and hidden strength of lesbian widows out of the closet."

Kathleen DeBold
Executive Director,
Mautner Project,
The National Lesbian
Health Organization

Lesbian Widows
Invisible Grief

Lesbian Widows
Invisible Grief

Vicky Whipple

HPP

Harrington Park Press®
An Imprint of The Haworth Press, Inc.
New York • London • Oxford

For more information on this book or to order, visit
http://www.haworthpress.com/store/product.asp?sku=5434

or call 1-800-HAWORTH (800-429-6784) in the United States and Canada
or (607) 722-5857 outside the United States and Canada

or contact orders@HaworthPress.com

Published by

Harrington Park Press®, an imprint of The Haworth Press, Inc., 10 Alice Street, Binghamton, NY 13904-1580.

PUBLISHER'S NOTES
The development, preparation, and publication of this work has been undertaken with great care. However, the Publisher, employees, editors, and agents of The Haworth Press are not responsible for any errors contained herein or for consequences that may ensue from use of materials or information contained in this work. The Haworth Press is committed to the dissemination of ideas and information according to the highest standards of intellectual freedom and the free exchange of ideas. Statements made and opinions expressed in this publication do not necessarily reflect the views of the Publisher, Directors, management, or staff of The Haworth Press, Inc., or an endorsement by them.

Most identities and circumstances of individuals discussed in this book have been changed to protect confidentiality. In a few cases, individuals have given permission to use their names and circumstances.

Cover design by Lora Wiggins.

Library of Congress Cataloging-in-Publication Data

Whipple, Vicky.
    Lesbian widows : invisible grief / Vicky Whipple.
        p. cm.
    Includes bibliographical references and index.
    ISBN-13: 978-1-56023-330-5 (hc. : alk. paper)
    ISBN-10: 1-56023-330-3 (hc. : alk. paper)
    ISBN-13: 978-1-56023-331-2 (pbk. : alk. paper)
    ISBN-10: 1-56023-331-1 (pbk. : alk. paper)
    1. Lesbians—Psychology. 2. Widows—Psychology. 3. Lesbian couples—Case studies. 4. Widowhood—Case studies. 5. Bereavement. 6. Grief. 7. Homophobia. I. Title.

HQ75.55.W45 2005
155.9'37'086643—dc22

                                                                           2005024814

This book is dedicated to MC
with gratitude for the time we shared.

ABOUT THE AUTHOR

Vicky Whipple, EdD, is an associate professor in the Counseling Department at National-Louis University where she has developed and taught a course on counseling LGBT clients. She is also a licensed clinical professional counselor in Illinois where she has had a private practice for the last fifteen years specializing in women's issues and the LGBT population. Dr. Whipple has published articles in professional journals and presented workshops at professional conferences on battered women, feminist family therapy, gender identity, and now lesbian widows. She is a member of the American Counseling Association and is a nationally certified counselor and an approved clinical supervisor. Dr. Whipple is also a clinical member and approved supervisor for the American Association for Marriage and Family Therapy.

CONTENTS

Preface

This book is based on a qualitative research study that I conducted as a participant-observer. Being a participant-observer means that I did this research and wrote this book as an insider. That is, I was a lesbian widow interviewing other lesbian widows. In qualitative research, objectivity is not the goal, and I most definitely was not able to be impartial about collecting widows' stories and writing this book. As a participant-observer, I was not emotionally removed from the topic, and I brought my own personal experience to the research.

Since I am a college professor, I went through appropriate channels at my university to obtain official sanction to conduct research using human subjects. All of the subsequent participants signed an informed consent form allowing me to use the information they sent me in this book, in journal articles, and in presentations at conferences. In this document I explained what I was doing and how I would use a pseudonym to protect their privacy if they wished. I also informed them of the risks involved, the primary one being that writing about the death of their partner would probably be emotionally stressful. But I also suggested that the benefits of participating would outweigh the risks. It could be cathartic for them as well as helpful to other lesbians who were widowed. Jane e-mailed me, saying, "Thank you for your work and the opportunity to possibly help others. You are right to say that the process of filling out the questionnaire is somewhat healing. Certainly it is thought-provoking."

I advertised in *Lesbian Connection* and other resources, asking for lesbian widows willing to complete a questionnaire or be interviewed about their experiences. Women contacted me mainly by e-mail, but also by telephone and letter. With the majority I engaged in at least one, and often several, interactions. Over the course of a year, I received responses from sixty-two women from all over the United States. In the end, twenty-four women, living in thirteen different states, followed through and completed a questionnaire.

One of the first women who contacted me happened to live only a couple of hours away from me, so I asked her if I could interview her in person. She had already written out her answers but agreed to the interview. I thought that the more women I could interview in person or by phone, the better. I was surprised to find otherwise. After interviewing Maureen, I transcribed the tape and discovered that she had basically told me verbally what she had already written. Plus, the interview had taken a great deal of time since we kept going off on tangents. I also found myself emotionally drained by the encounter.

In addition to this experience of interviewing one widow in person, I found that when I offered the opportunity to be interviewed, the women who contacted me preferred to write their responses to the questionnaire or to make audiotapes of their answers. No one wanted to be interviewed in person, I think because they knew it would be too emotional for them. I had a graduate student assist me with transcribing some of the tapes sent to me, and she said that the women on the tapes kept stopping and crying. Although relying on written or taped responses created some problems, that is, not everyone answered every question, I believe each widow shared the essence of her experience and what she thought might be helpful to others.

I invited participants to answer five general questions in their own words. Based on Seidman's (1991) guidelines for phenomenological interviewing, I first asked them to tell me the story of their relationship so that I might have a sense of the context in which they had lived together. (Thus, the internal validity or consistency of the research was enhanced.) I asked them to tell me about the illness, if any, and death of their partner. I wanted to know about their own grief journey afterward, including what or who helped them and what or who was not helpful. I asked how long it had been since their partner had died and where they thought they were now emotionally in the grief recovery process. Finally, I wanted to know what they believed they had learned from this experience and what advice they might give to others in the same situation.

I deliberately chose to let participants answer each question with as much or as little information as they wished, believing that they would share what was most important to them. For example, I did not ask specifically about the ethnicity of these lesbian widows, and only one, born in a South American country, mentioned it. I have assumed that meant that everyone else was white. Regarding the ethnicity of deceased partners, one widow described her partner as "Tex-Mex" and another had a partner from South America. My assumption, again, would be that the remainder were white. That assumption, however, may be incorrect.

My former partner was only forty-six years old when she died, highly respected in her profession, well-loved by family and friends. The ages of the partners of the women who contacted me ranged from thirty to sixty-nine at the time of their deaths, the majority in their fifties when they died. I was fifty-two at the time of my partner's death. The ages of the other widows in this book ranged from twenty-nine to sixty-six years old, with the majority in their forties. Thus, part of what we share in this book is the pain of being widowed too young, and of having a lover who died in the prime of life. My speculation is that lesbians who were older (over seventy-five years of age) and whose partners died at an older age did not contact me because they had lived their lives in the closet. Even though they were guaranteed confidentiality, they were uncomfortable talking about their lives openly. But that is only guesswork on my part.

Of the twenty-four widows who shared their stories in this book, five experienced the sudden, unexpected death of their partner. One was shot; one died in a car accident; one had a massive heart attack; another a cerebral hemorrhage; and one died in her sleep. The remainder, like me, had a partner who died slowly of an illness or complications from surgery. Fourteen of the nineteen partners in the latter category died of some form of cancer.

In asking about their relationship, I identified the length of time each couple had spent together prior to the death of one partner. There was a range of five months to thirty-seven years. Yet it seemed to me that the amount of time that lesbian partners had spent together did not seem to make a difference in the amount of anguish that was experienced. Many survivors used a term such as *soul mate* to speak of their deceased life partner, indicating the depth of the connection they felt. One widow had been partnered for only five months but felt that she had lost the love of her life. Only eight of the twenty-four relationships, one-third, had lasted less than five years. Emily and I had been together nearly seven years, and the majority of women in this book had spent from six to twenty years together as a couple. Three relationships had lasted over thirty years: thirty-seven, thirty-two, and thirty-one years respectively. Thus the stories in this book involve women in long-term, deeply committed relationships.

The amount of time that had elapsed since the partner's death was also varied. I discouraged women who had been widowed less than a year from answering the questionnaire because their feelings were still so raw. But three women who had been widowed less than a year insisted on participating anyway. Three more wrote after having been widowed for less than two years. An additional eleven had been widowed from two to five years, and three more from six to ten years. There were four widows for whom there was a considerable time lapse: twelve, thirteen, fifteen, and seventeen years respectively. I had anticipated that the greater the amount of time since the death of the partner, the less emotional their answers to the questionnaire would sound. But I was wrong. Those whose partner had passed away more than ten years previously may have provided less detail about the circumstances of the partner's death, but I could still hear the pain of the experience in what they wrote.

An interesting discovery I made as I read these women's stories was that, like me, one-fourth of those who responded had experienced the death of another significant person in their life around the same time that their partner died. Some, like me, had lost a parent; one had a child who had died in the previous year; and another lost a sister. This double loss complicated our grief recovery (Worden, 2002). In my case, although I missed my mother, it was more than two years after Emily's death before I began truly mourning the loss of my mother.

Another remarkable finding was that half of the widows who contacted me or their deceased partners (forty-eight women altogether) had previously been married. One of the reasons that I felt I needed to include the stories of other widows in this book was that I had previously been married and had children and grandchildren. I thought my story would be different from those of other lesbians. I had not anticipated that so many other widows or their deceased partners would have been previously married.

I make no claim that the experiences shared in this book are representative of all lesbians. That is not the purpose of qualitative research, for one thing. Another consideration is that the lesbian community in general is quite diverse, as noted in Chapter 15, "For Professionals." In addition, the majority of widows who contacted me responded to one of my ads in *Lesbian Connection*. A few heard about the ads from friends who received *Lesbian Connection*. One woman responded to a solicitation on a professional LISTSERV mailing list, and one responded after personal contact at a Golden Threads festival. This is not a scientific random survey of participants and, therefore, represents only that segment of lesbian widows who received information about my project, decided to respond, and then followed through by signing the informed consent document and completing the questionnaire.

Although I did not begin to formally analyze the data (the participants' answers to my questionnaire) until all questionnaires were completed, by then I had already noticed, as I read their stories, that the patterns and themes emerging indicated many commonalities. This, plus my discovery that these themes were echoed in grief books, helped to affirm the external validity of this research (Seidman, 1991). I have organized the chapters to reflect themes that I noticed in our stories.

Chapter 1 provides an overview of this project, followed by Chapter 2, which opens with my personal story of shock at being told that Emily had a terminal illness. I then relate the stories of the five lesbians whose partner died unexpectedly and the shock they experienced when they were told that their partner had passed away. Chapters 3, 4, and 5 include the stories of the remaining nineteen widows whose partner died after a period of illness. Chapter 3 explores the sense of continued disbelief after a partner was diagnosed with a terminal illness. Chapter 4 shares the stories of five women who became involved with lesbians who already had a long-term illness, and Chapter 5 is devoted to describing the time that widows spent taking care of their partner before she died, including the emotional and physical exhaustion of being a caretaker.

In Chapter 6, you will find stories of what we experienced in the last moments of our lover's life, while in Chapter 7 we share the creative ways we designed funerals or memorial services. Chapter 8 describes how painful the first few months after our partner's death were for us. In Chapter 9, I recount where we found comfort and support, while Chapter 10 relates three areas that complicated our recovery: legal hassles, the lack of professional support services, and the lack of written materials specifically for lesbians. Chapter 11 gives an overview of our experiences within the first two years after our partner died, the time when the pain of our loss was most intense. Chapter 12 contains information about what it was like to find a new love and the difficulties we faced in beginning a new relationship. In Chapter 13, we share our perspectives on grief from the sixth month through the seventeenth year after a partner's death. Chapter 14 includes advice to family and friends about what they can do to be supportive of us in our grief recovery process. Chapter 15 is directed to professionals.

I and the twenty-four widows who graciously contributed their experience to this book hope that sharing our stories is a source of comfort and guidance to those who unfortunately join us on this pilgrimage of grief, as well as a resource of information for the families, friends, and professionals who support them.

Acknowledgments

I would like to express my appreciation to the twenty-four widows who entrusted me with their stories and contributed to this book. Having experienced the pain of being widowed and finding no written resources specifically for lesbians, you agreed with me that a book needed to be written. Thank you for making that possible.

My deep gratitude goes to Carolyn and Diana. Not only were you part of my support system during and after Em's death, but also, from the moment I mentioned writing a book, you have been supportive and encouraging. Thank you also, Carolyn, for giving me early feedback as I began writing the book. My thanks too to Juanita for reading my first draft and giving me feedback.

I must extend a thank-you to Jim Ellor, who was my colleague at National-Louis University during the time I wrote this book. Thank you, Jim, for writing a supportive letter for me to The Haworth Press. My thanks also go to the administration, faculty, and staff at National-Louis who supported me in this endeavor, especially Susan Thorne-Devin, my department chair at the time.

I am grateful to Reverend Linda and partner Toni for their unending support. I would also like to thank my HOWLs (Hilarious Older Wiser Lesbians) friends and my women's spirituality group. You helped me rebuild my life, and I appreciate your friendship. My gratitude, as well as that of many other lesbian widows in this book, goes to the Hospice Foundation of America. You were the one organization who recognized our pain and did what you could to support us. In particular, I want to thank my hospice volunteer, Sue Hardy, for listening to and befriending me during one of the darkest hours of my life.

I am so grateful for your love and support, Carole (pseudonym). You helped me discover that I could love again and have been unfailing in your encouragement as I have labored on this book. And last, but certainly not least, I want to thank Kathy Nedrow. We have known each other since first grade, and I could not ask for a better friend. Thank you.

Chapter 1

Introduction

While the rest of the country celebrated the arrival of a new millennium on December 31, 1999, I was at home wondering if I was going to have to rush Emily to the emergency room of the hospital again. She had been complaining about stomach pain and difficulty eating for several months, but doctors could not figure out why. She was scheduled to be admitted into the hospital for some procedures after the holidays, but that New Year's Eve she was in so much pain that we cancelled our plans to get together with friends and hoped that we would soon have some answers.

A few days later, I was sitting in a hospital waiting room when the surgeon walked in to inform us that Emily had cancer, a deadly form of stomach cancer. Life expectancy? Less than a year. Words cannot describe what I felt in that moment: *This can't be happening; I must be dreaming. Somebody wake me up.* But this was the beginning of a ten-month nightmare of watching Em waste away and die.

This sense of shock, this feeling of living in a nightmare, was emphasized to me over and over by the other women who share their stories in this book. It was a central, defining moment in my life and theirs. In my situation, losing Em was the beginning of a series of life-changing experiences. One month after her death, I moved out of our home to a new location, and three weeks later my mother passed away unexpectedly. At that point I had been a professional counselor for sixteen years and a counselor educator for two. I had training in grief counseling and had worked with two lesbians who had lost their partners. One was still experiencing posttraumatic stress ten years after her lover was killed in a hate crime. The other had actually experienced the death of two partners, one in a tragic accident and one from cancer. But all that textbook learning and professional experience did not prepare me to face the pain of the death of two of the most important people in my life.

Shirley, one of the widows whose stories are included in this book, made a similar comment. She is a social worker in a nursing home.

> Isn't it strange how we work with death and dying daily (I do anyway with the geriatric population) and yet when it pertains to our personal life, we are unable to know what to do or how to do it?

THE DECISION TO WRITE

I was fortunate to find support services through my local hospice to help me deal with my grief. I also read many books from their library but soon realized that no book about lesbian widows existed. I began to think about writing one myself. However, I felt that just sharing my personal story would not be enough to create a book that was meaningful to other lesbians who had been widowed, so I advertised for lesbian widows willing to complete a questionnaire or be interviewed about their experiences. When women responded, they wanted to know why I was looking for lesbian widows and what I was going to do with the information. They would express their sympathy when they heard that I had recently been widowed. Some offered me comfort and advice. For example, when I e-mailed Pat to apologize for not responding to her sooner, I explained that I had just gone through the first anniversary of Emily's death and that it had been a very difficult time for me. She e-mailed back:

> I know that each passing anniversary of Emily's death will be different for you. Difficult but different. You will always miss her, but it does get easier on a day-to-day basis. Betty has been gone now for three years, and I regularly marvel at how drastically my life has changed.

Many widows also commented to me that it felt wonderful to talk to someone who really understood what they had gone through. Most had never met another lesbian who had been widowed. Every single one was excited about my writing a book. They too had discovered that there were hardly any resources available to lesbians on this subject. A few of them had even considered writing their own book but had found it emotionally too difficult to do. So they cheered me on, anxious to see the results.

BOOK PARTICIPANTS

I changed the names of all the women who participated in this project except for the five who gave me permission to use their real names: Beverly, Irene, Lois, Shirley, and Joy. For me personally, what I share about myself is true, but Emily (pseudonym) was not out when she was alive, except to a select group of lesbian friends, and I believe it would dishonor her memory to out her now. I have, therefore, disguised information about her. I have also given my current partner the pseudonym Carole to protect her privacy.

Any woman, straight or gay, who is widowed experiences a great deal of emotional pain from the loss, but lesbian widows are confronted with additional challenges that are not a part of the grief process of married widows. The lack of public recognition of our relationships, the lack of professional support services, and legal and financial difficulties because our relationships are not recognized as marriages are unique to us as lesbians. In my determination to write this book, I had not realized that I would end up making a case for gay marriage. However, the experiences of discrimination that we faced provide concrete examples of the injustices that happen when gays and lesbians are not allowed to legally marry.

In addition to legal and financial discrimination, none of us could see ourselves or our experiences in the pages of grief books. Either books had stories of married widows or they addressed the issues of gay men whose partners died of AIDS. Although the relationships of gay men, like lesbian relationships, tend to be invisible in our society, and there are, therefore, some commonalities between us, reading about AIDS deaths still did not speak to our specific issues. Heather shared her frustration in finding no grief book for lesbians:

> I did not find much on this topic [lesbian widows] ten to twelve years ago when I looked. Once things started getting really bad with AIDS, I started seeing more, but of course most of it was focused on men.

My original plan in writing this book was to elaborate on how we recovered from losing a partner and created a new life without her so that future lesbian widows would have some guidelines and support. But every single participant wrote more about their relationship and the trauma of the death itself than about their recovery process.

Three-fourths of the pages containing their stories were focused on their relationship with and then the deaths of their partner. At first I was disappointed. I did not want this book to be just a collection of stories. I wanted it to have answers that would be helpful to others. But then I realized how the very fact that everyone focused more on sharing the life and death of their partner than on their own grief journey held a message in and of itself. We were traumatized by the death of our loved one. It is in telling our story that we recover; it is in sharing our experience that we help others to heal.

This book is not a comprehensive resource on grief. Other books, such as those listed in the bibliography, provide more in-depth explanations of grief and mourning. Rather, this book is a resource in which lesbians who are widowed can read about women like themselves, where they can see their own experience on the written page. In other words, the purpose of this book is to help end our invisibility. I kept a journal during Em's illness and in the years since her death, and I have been able to draw on that information for this book. In each chapter, I quote from my journal and the stories of the other twenty-four lesbian widows as much as possible.

WRITING FROM EXPERIENCE

Even though I had training in grief counseling, I knew that knowledge of grief was not the same as experiencing grief. I also knew that, in order to recover, I had to put aside my professional understanding and allow myself to feel pain. That was also how I worked with the experiences of the other lesbian widows included in this book. I considered our stories to be the truth of experts. After all, we were the ones who had lived through it. To write this book, I first outlined what I learned from the lesbian widows themselves. It was only later, as I was finalizing what to include in each chapter of this book, that I began to add commentary from other grief books.

Grief, we are told, "is a normal and natural reaction to loss of any kind" (James and Friedman, 1998, p. 3). Some authors differentiate between grief and mourning, but in this book I use the terms *grieving* and *mourning* interchangeably. American culture makes it difficult to mourn. Showing emotion in public is frowned upon, and we are expected to get it as quickly as possible. Even mental health professionals do not necessarily understand grief. The classic model that was taught for years was that a person could experience shock and intense grief for two weeks, and then take up to two more years to conclude the mourning process (Becvar, 2001). As you read our stories, you will see that grief never really ends; its pain only lessens over time.

I collected the stories of the twenty-four lesbian widows in this book during the second year after Emily's death. My own emotions were still pretty raw and I cried my way through reading each story sent to me, reliving my own painful experience. There were days when I could work on this project and be okay, and then other days when I wondered why in the world I had started this. It was just too painful. I know that the women who share their stories in this book had a similar experience. It was painful to remember, to write, to speak about their experiences, but they too felt a need to provide something for the lesbian community. Using my experience and that of the other widows, I then wrote this book during the third and fourth years after Emily died. I could tell that I had a little more emotional distance, but there were still times when it was difficult to work on it. In fact, as I was proofreading the final copy of this book, I had a series of dreams, nightmares really, that were very upsetting, but I did not understand what they were about. My current partner was the one who said, "Are you afraid of losing something or someone?" Bingo. In working on the book, I found myself fearing that something would happen to Carole and I would once again be widowed.

LESBIAN RELATIONSHIPS

To understand the significance of our loss, I think it is important to talk about the kind and quality of relationship that exists between two women. Two women in a relationship tend to experience a deep emotional connection. In the past, some therapists pathologized lesbian relationships for being too close, too enmeshed. That was because they were comparing lesbian relationships to heterosexual relationships. The quality of a relationship between two women tends to be more intense than that of a male-female relationship, not in a pathological way but in a way that is deeply satisfying to the women involved (Ossana, 2000). There is a sense of intimacy within lesbian relationships that is emotionally gratifying to both partners. One nationwide study indicated that 95 percent of lesbians who participated in that particular research project expressed the hope that they would grow old together with their current partner (Walter, 2003). This suggests another reason why the news of the terminal illness or death of a lesbian partner is so traumatic: Both women's lives and futures were emotionally invested in their relationship.

In addition to the difference in the very nature of the relationship of two women and the emotional investment women make in their relationships, heterosexism and homophobia act as catalysts to draw lesbian partners even closer together as a defense against the world's hostility. Heterosexism, the belief that everyone is and must be heterosexual, results in lesbian relationships being invisible and unrecognized in the world at large. Heterosexism and homophobia, fear of gays and lesbians, are at the root of verbal and physical violence against gays and lesbians. Lesbian couples must create a home life and a support network that counteract these negative messages from society. This further reinforces the already close nature of lesbian relationships.

When I began a new relationship with Carole during the time I was writing this book, a friend asked me if I was still going to write my book, thinking, I guess, that it would not be important to me to finish it since I had apparently moved on with my life. But there was absolutely no question in my mind that I was going to write and publish this book. I could not disappoint all the women who had sent their stories to me and applauded my effort. It was a book that had to be written. It is the book that I and the other twenty-four widows who contributed their stories wish we could have had to read when our partner died. Marilyn, one of the widows included in this book, stated the need for it this way:

> As more of our sisters become committed partners and mothers, there will be more of us who sadly also experience widowhood. As the rest of the world begins to understand our love as something more than a sexual attraction that can be satisfied by any one-night stand, but rather as fully committed and lovingly intimate relationships, they may also come to recognize the extent of our grief, the depth of our loss.

Until our relationships are recognized legally, our partnerships, our losses, and our grief will remain invisible. My hope is that this book is one step toward ending that invisibility.

Chapter 2

Shock and Denial

Mine is not the typical coming-out story. I am one of those late bloomers who did not discover my attraction to women until I was in my forties. By then I had been married more than twenty years, was in the process of getting divorced, and had two adult children and two grandchildren. For a long time I wondered if I was a "real" lesbian, but, over time, I met many other previously married women who had also come out in midlife. And then when my partner died, I decided that even if some lesbians had trouble accepting formerly married women into their community, I had paid my dues, so to speak.

Emily was the first woman for whom I was able to clearly identify my feelings as more than friendship. We met and became friends through a series of feminist meetings that culminated in the establishment of a local women's center. I found myself falling head over heels in love with her. At the time we met, Em was a college professor and I was a professional counselor with a private practice. Our feminist principles and spiritual leanings were similar, and I felt that we were soul mates.

We were both in the closet at work and with our families, but over time we discreetly became friends with other lesbians who lived near us. We worked together at the women's center and enjoyed golfing with our friends. With Em's encouragement and support, I applied for a teaching position at a different university and was hired to train master's-level mental health counselors. Like all couples, we had our rocky times to work through, but after a few years we adopted the image of growing old together, sitting in our rocking chairs on the front porch, sipping tea.

About a year before she died, Emily began experiencing abdominal pain and difficulty eating. She had always been resistant to seeking medical help, and it took months before she agreed to make a doctor's appointment. The first doctor ruled out her gallbladder as the source of the problem and treated her for acid reflux disease, to no avail. Another doctor suggested it was an ulcer and put her on medication, which also did not help. Gradually the pain disrupted her sleep and she needed to nap during the day. Over a three-month period, she lost more than thirty pounds on an already slim frame.

Several times, as I looked at her as she was napping, I had this eerie sense of seeing her lying in a casket. I told myself to stop being morbid, that of course she would be okay, but the thought lingered. Looking back now, it seems that feeling was a premonition. The night before an endoscopy was scheduled, a friend stopped to visit. She was upset that a colleague of hers had just been given six months to live. We each shared what we would do if we had only six months to live, never thinking that would be exactly what Em would soon be facing. Her wish that night was to have time with family and friends, and she was, indeed, granted her wish.

The endoscopy discovered a blockage at the bottom of her stomach; the doctor sampled the tissue, and tests showed it was not cancerous. Relief. Two days later the surgeon operated to remove the blockage. I will always be able to relive that night in my mind. Sitting in the waiting room with friends and family, the surgery taking over four hours instead of the one and a half the doctor had predicted. The doctor walking in and saying it was cancer, stage III stomach cancer. He had removed 75 percent of Em's stomach and the surrounding lymph nodes. She had maybe a year to live. With chemotherapy and radiation her life might be prolonged another year, but this cancer was fatal. I wept openly and unashamedly. One day I was told it was not cancer; two days later she was dying from cancer. I asked friends to take me home that night because I could not trust myself to drive. That night I wrote in my journal:

I am in shock. It is just unbelievable. How can I go ahead with life as usual? Thank God for supportive friends. Em will be devastated when she wakes up and finds out. I thought that when I had to deal with Steve's [my son's] mental illness that it was a living hell and nothing worse could possibly happen. But facing cancer and death with Em will win the prize.

Six days after her initial surgery, I had a phone message waiting for me when I arrived at work saying that Em had been rushed into the operating room to repair a popped stitch and deal with pancreatitis. Then she developed pneumonia and had a high fever. She spent days in intensive care, her life hanging in the balance.

We just were not prepared for this at all. Even though I finally slept last night, I feel exhausted. Please don't let her die, please give us time. [Em had always called herself a Pollyanna.] Maybe I am the Pollyanna now. I was totally unprepared for a diagnosis of cancer and I do not want to believe now that she won't fight this and live.

For the next ten months, Emily endured repeated hospital visits and medical procedures, and I did what seemed to me like endless caretaking. My minister was surprised that I had been so unprepared to deal with the possibility of Emily dying. She had tried to address the subject with me before Em went into the hospital, but I did not want to listen. A couple weeks after Emily's initial surgery, I wrote,

I think I am still in shock and still can't believe this is really happening. This is a nightmare. Somebody please wake me up. In a dream I had last night, I was part of an army involved in a war, but I didn't have a weapon to fight with. That seems apropos—I have no way to defend myself from this.

Although I was faced with the shock of a death sentence for my partner, I still had ten months to prepare for Em's death. Other lesbian widows were not that fortunate. Those women whose partner died unexpectedly could recall in detail the day and time and circumstances of their partner's deaths. Their sense of shock was poignant.

ELLEN AND KATE

Ellen and Kate met when a mutual friend of theirs was hospitalized. Ellen was going through a divorce. She explained what decisions she had reached in her life at that time:

I did not know how things would work out for me but I knew that (1) I would never again settle for less than devoted love, (2) the children (ages eight and ten) were my absolute first priority, and (3) I probably wanted to be with women.

I fell in love with Kate as we met to pray for our friend's healing. Our spiritual connection remained a strong theme throughout our relationship, and this was very important to both of us. Our attraction for each other was intense and passionate, and this also remained very strong (though a little more reasonable than those first few months!). Kate moved in with me and we began to build our wonderful home life together.

Kate had a small accounting practice and we expanded our home to expand her office. Kate fully participated as a stepmom. She told me it had always been her dream to have children.

Ellen and Kate, along with Ellen's two children, were on vacation in Hawaii when Kate died. They had just enjoyed a wonderful dinner and Kate was driving all of them back to the hotel when the unthinkable happened. Ellen sent me this selection from her diary to describe it:

I looked up suddenly as Kate muttered something. Lights are heading toward us. Headlights are veering across the center line into our lane. Kate cuts the wheel as much as she can. I feel the crash but I'm blinded by something, the airbag. I feel pushed hard. I am crushed against the door. I hear screams and I am very confused for a moment, as if I am in a cloud. My right arm hurt but I knew that I was OK. I hear screams from my son, "Get out of the car! Get out of the car!" I fumble for the seatbelt and the door handle. Finally I stumble out.

Where is Kate? I turned around and saw that the driver's side was crushed in. Kate is pinned by the windshield and steering wheel. She is unconscious, her head is turned to the side, there is blood flowing down her neck and chest. I am an RN and should know something about emergencies, but I lose my mind. I screamed and screamed, "Help us now! Someone help us!" My children were clinging to me, and we were all crying together.

Firefighters arrived and told us to get away from the car. "Don't move her, don't touch her!" they said. "Get away from the car; it might still explode!" I refused. "No! No, I won't move her but I won't leave her!" But they made me leave. I thought to myself, "They will take Kate to the hospital. She is hurt badly but she'll pull through. Kate is strong. We love her so much. We need her." Then I looked back at the car. A sheet was pulled over her. "What is going on?" The paramedic tells me that Kate is dead. "She died quickly," he said, "of massive injuries." "NO! NO! NO! This is a nightmare. It can't be true. No, it's not true!"

Ellen and Kate had been partners for six and a half years at the time Kate died so tragically. In describing the loving life that they had built together, Ellen wrote, "Ugh, this sounds so dry and lifeless. . . . And Kate was so the opposite of that. She was so full of life. Playful and funny and passionate and silly and so much more."

JANET AND CHRIS

Ellen, like me, had this sense of being in a nightmare. Janet described her experience a little differently, that life was colorless and without meaning when Chris died. Janet worked as a paramedic with the fire department and Chris was a police officer. They had met eight years previously in an emergency room when they were both filling out paperwork in the line of duty. Janet explained,

> I liked my life and was doing lots of things, which did not leave me with much time to date nor to look. My friends said they had met someone who was just perfect for me. I laughed . . . loud and hard. I knew I was finicky and picky to the max. And doubled with the fact that I don't do blind dates, I laughed that much harder. We had several friends in common, and they were telling her about me and me about her.
>
> While filling out the paperwork at the hospital that day, I kept thinking about the great legs on this police officer, and went to ask a nurse friend if she might know who belonged to the long brown hair and great legs. She laughed and said she was the person they had tried to set me up with!

Janet explained that, during their eight years together, they had few things in common but they made each other laugh and enjoyed each other's company.

> I can remember the tingling feeling I would get when she walked into the room. We both knew we were going to grow old wrapped inside each other's arms and never stop laughing and learning. My days and nights became filled with awesome laughter and love. We truly enjoyed each other. Friends could see just by looking; they said that we glowed and our laughter was infectious.

Janet was wondering why Chris was late getting home from work one day when she heard the doorbell ring and saw a squad car parked outside.

> My heart sank and at that moment I felt like I was going in slow motion. I ran to the door to find the captain standing with a blank colorless face on. I didn't stop to let him open his mouth to explain, I just grabbed him and ran to the car as he explained on the way. All he could do was tear up and say that she was shot and they did not know her condition. We went full tilt, red lights and screaming sirens.

Four hundred million things going through my mind, all the things which I wanted to tell her, and that I would, as soon as I saw her. Little did I know that I would never get the chance. She was gone. She died before we got to the hospital. The rage, resentment, and disgust I had welling up inside me for not being the responding unit, for not being there to say "I love you." What happened? Why? Why wasn't I called and all the other why's. (My mother swore up and down that she should have tattooed that "WHY" word on my forehead.)

In the following few hours, making all the decisions was mind-boggling. I knew what she wanted in a roundabout way as we had somewhere in the million small conversations talked about the "what ifs," but you never think you will really have to deal with it. The department chaplain came in and said words which seemed faint. We were a couple but we had no official paperwork and marriage was out. I can't remember all the bazillion questions they needed answers to right at that moment; I can't recall if I even answered. I felt life, my life, was a flat colorless photo with no dimensions and no life. Life was gone and who to turn to was a blur. I felt the cold wrap around me and I knew nothing was going to be able to warm me up.

Friends and co-workers had no real idea of what was going on in my head. I felt so incredibly alone and lost. At thirty, my life ended the moment Chris was gone. No one to share the good times with or laugh at the bad hair days. Everything looked lifeless, no color, just a bad distorted black-and-white photo.

ANITA AND HOLLY

Thirty years old is too young to be a widow. Being widowed is supposed to be for elderly people. Tragically, however, Janet was, indeed, widowed at age thirty. Anita also experienced the sudden, unexpected death of her partner. Anita and Holly did not live together; they commuted two hours to spend time with each other.

Our life together for the most part was just wonderful, even though we both had to commute on the weekends to see each other. I had a position in academia as a professor, so I had the summers off and a lot of the holidays so I went to her house more than she came to mine. And besides, she had her mother to watch, so she had to make sure if she came on a Friday night that she left early Sunday morning and that put a little cramp on our relationship, but we worked it out. When we wanted to go on vacation, she used to hire someone to look in on her mother. Holly and I traveled quite a bit. We went to Mexico and South Dakota and saw Mt. Rushmore and the Grand Canyon. We loved to travel together. Had good times.

We really didn't talk about our future much because Holly was younger than me. I was about twelve years older. Retirement was still a ways off, so we never talked about our plans. Her mother died in 1998, and that was very hard on Holly. After Holly's mother died, well, even before that, Holly began to drink. I was not expecting that because I thought it was time for "us" now.

Holly was not out formally to her brother and his wife and adult children living in Florida. She used to go there during the winter holiday but never invited me because she was not out to them. I am out with my family but we could not talk about that with her family. They probably knew, but it was a subject to be avoided and that really made it very cumbersome. In fact, when Holly died, her brother and his wife did not even talk to me. They sold her house and auctioned off all her belongings without telling me. I gave her many things and at least I could have had those back as a memento. My friends had to tell me, and I was just so terribly sad and angry, frustrated.

Holly died unexpectedly. She was, as far as I know, healthy except that she did drink a lot. It happened at six o'clock at night. She was talking on the phone with her brother and fell right off of the chair. She was all alone, so her brother called a friend of hers and had her go to the house to see what happened to Holly.

Of course I was not prepared when I got the phone call the next morning. I did not believe it. Her friend told me Holly was in the hospital, and I thought to myself that she would be all right. What her friend did not tell me at the time was that Holly was on a ventilator, brain dead. She died of a massive cerebral hemorrhage to the brain, very quickly.

CASSIE AND FRAN

Imagine Anita's shock when, after driving two hours, she arrived at the hospital to be told that Holly had already died. She was not the only one, however, to be faced with the unbelievable. Cassie wrote this visually descriptive account of the shock she felt the day her partner, Fran, died unexpectedly:

IT WAS A MORNING NOT LIKE ANY OTHER MORNING
IT WAS THE *WORST* MORNING IN MY LIFE EVER
WORSE THAN THE MORNING WE LEFT BUENOS AIRES.
AT TEN, MY ROOTS WERE SEVERED. THAT MORNING
IT WOULD TAKE A LONG TIME TO RECOVER FROM
   THAT DEPARTURE ON THAT MORNING
UNTIL *THAT* MORNING

IT WAS NOT LIKE ANY OTHER MORNING
IT WAS THE *WORST* MORNING IN MY LIFE EVER.
WORSE THAN THE MORNING I KNEW FOR SURE
AT 26, I HAD INHERITED THE FAMILY DISEASE.
AND FROM THAT MORNING ON AND EVERY
   MORNING AFTER THAT DIABETES WOULD
   DOMINATE MY FIRST THOUGHT EVERY MORNING
UNTIL *THAT* MORNING

IT WAS NOT A MORNING LIKE ANY OTHER MORNING
IT WAS THE *WORST* MORNING IN MY LIFE EVER
WORSE THAN THE MORNING I HAD TO SIT DOWN
TO HEAL A FOOT FROM DIABETIC COMPLICATIONS
AND DUE TO MORE COMPLICATIONS ONE MORNING
I KNEW I WOULD USE AN ELECTRIC SCOOTER FOR
   MOBILITY
EVERY MORNING FROM THAT MORNING ON
UNTIL *THAT* MORNING

IT WAS NOT A MORNING LIKE ANY OTHER MORNING
IT WAS THE *WORST* MORNING OF MY LIFE EVER
WORSE THAN THE MORNING THAT I ACKNOWLEDGED
MY EARLY RETIREMENT FROM SINGING
AND MORNINGS BECAME MORE DIFFICULT

WITHOUT THAT PURPOSE I WOKE UP EACH MORNING FOR
UNTIL *THAT* MORNING

Cassie shared the following about her relationship with Fran and how Fran died:

Fran and I had found each other nine months earlier and knew instantly we were soul mates, ready to spend the rest of our lives together. We each wore each other's engagement ring. I woke up around five that morning, totally delighted that Fran was lying next to me. Fran was lying on her back, and in that instant of delight, it did not occur to me that this was unusual. Fran always slept on her right side with her back to me due to an injury to her back at work. It was not until I returned from the bathroom, slipped gently back into bed, and took her hand that I began to feel that this was unusual.

When I took her hand and she did not move is when it dawned on me that she was on her back! *What's up?* I thought. I held my breath and nudged her slightly. There was no response whatsoever and then I nudged a bit harder. Again there was no response and that is when I called out her name. That is when my delightful morning became the *morning not like any other morning ever.*

I called the paramedics immediately, with a panic I had never felt before. "Do mouth to mouth resuscitation while the paramedics are on their way," I sort of heard the operator say over the speakerphone. I tried to follow her instructions with the greatest of care. I could not believe what was happening. Instead of kissing my sweetheart, my lover with the eyes and smile of an angel, the one I had searched for all these years, the most honorable and handsome Tex-Mex I had ever met, I was desperately trying to breathe life into her.

"He died of heart failure" was what the paramedic told me. In my despair, I corrected him immediately, "She." Did she suffer? What were her last moments like? Why didn't I wake up? I will never know. I do know that she died happy because she was next to me and we were happy together, even with our little struggles.

SHIRLEY AND TERRY

I could relate to Cassie's sense of shock. So could Shirley. Shirley contacted me six months after Terry died suddenly of a heart attack. Even though it was a short time since she had become a widow, Shirley insisted that she wanted to answer my questionnaire. I shared my story with her and we talked about which was worse—losing your partner suddenly or watching your partner die a slow death. She wrote,

> Terry was my first female lover. I had two previous marriages— ten years in each of them—four children and four stepchildren. Terry owned and operated a daycare in our home. She loved children and lived the childhood she never had through them. She was originally from New York, but loved Nebraska for the quiet and peacefulness it brought to her. She blossomed here and became her own person. Terry was thirty-eight when she died, sixteen years my junior.
>
> She died of a massive heart attack on March 1, 2002. On the night of February 28, we went to bed and made love. A half hour later, she was dead. She was in the bathroom, coughing and short of breath and refusing to see a doctor. By the time she agreed to let me call for help, it was too late. She fell off the toilet and died on the bathroom floor. My daughter and I administered CPR, but to no avail. When the paramedics came, they also tried, but it was no use. She was pronounced dead at the hospital.
>
> I remember being so angry with her for leaving me and not taking care of herself. She had been diagnosed as a borderline diabetic a few years earlier. She refused to check her blood sugar or even watch her diet. She was somewhat overweight and smoked a couple of packs of cigarettes every day. So, my anger was legitimate as far as I was concerned. I did not have the trauma of watching her die slowly as you did. I wonder which way is worse.

WHICH IS WORSE?

Of course there is no answer to the question, "Which is worse?" Both sudden and prolonged deaths are tragic and hurt deeply. The difference between a sudden death and one that has been anticipated is not in the amount of pain that we feel but in the ability to prepare for the death. I know that I began grieving from the moment I heard about Em's fatal diagnosis. Those who lost their partner unexpectedly experienced the same kind of pain at the moment they were told that their partner had died, but they were deprived of the opportunity I had to prepare for Emily's death and say good-bye. On the other hand, they did not have to watch their partner waste away and suffer over an extended period.

It is because our pain is so intense that one of our first reactions to learning that our partner is dying or has already passed away is shock. This shock is a normal and healthy reaction to our loss. It protects us from the full impact of the reality before us. We may feel we are in a dream or walking around in a fog. This sense of unreality enables us to live through this difficult time.

Ellen, Janet, Anita, Shirley, and Cassie did not have time to prepare for the death of their partner; shock hit them full force when they were told that their beloved had passed away. The widows in the next two chapters will share how, even though their partner did not die suddenly, there was still a sense of disbelief as they watched their partner become ill and die.

Chapter 3

Terminal Illness and Disbelief

Many times throughout the ten months of Emily's illness, I wrote in my journal about my disbelief. For others whose partner suffered through a long illness, the sense of shock and unreality also continued over time. We wanted to believe that somehow our partner would survive and beat the odds. Our denial was like emotional anesthesia that protected us as we saw our partner's life slipping away.

ANNA MARIE AND CAROLINE

Like my life partner, Caroline was diagnosed with stomach cancer. Like me, her partner, Anna Marie, kept hoping that Caroline would live. Here is their story.

Caroline was thirty-six and I was thirty-eight when we became lovers. We were together for seven years, but the beginning of our relationship was very rocky. Caroline was married and had two children. She got divorced, we started dating, and she moved in shortly after. For a while her daughter and then later her son moved in with us but returned to live with their father. I had been living by myself for five years, so I was not used to having people around.

After months of looking, Caroline found a job with the school district as a teacher's aide. She loved it and enjoyed the children. Everyone that I worked with knew that I was a lesbian. If they did not like me, then that was their problem. Caroline, however, was not out at school. But that is something that everybody has to do on their own, to decide whether or not to come out.

Caroline had been sick to her stomach a lot for a couple months. She finally was so ill one day, I took her to the hospital and spent all day at the emergency room. They discovered she had cancer. Later that day they had removed her stomach, one ovary, and several of the lymph nodes. She was in intensive care for a few days and then went to a regular room and then I got to bring her home.

Caroline had no insurance and we did not know what we were going to do. We had a couple friends, lesbian friends, who worked in Public Aid and we called them. They were very good. They came over and brought all the paperwork. The first thing they told me to do was to take her name off my checking account because otherwise I would end up paying a lot of bills. So they helped Caroline fill out all these papers. They got her food stamps and I guess you call it the green card or medical card, which paid for her medical expenses. That was really a godsend because I do not know how we would have paid for all this stuff. They were very helpful.

A couple months later, I had to take her to the hospital again because she was not eating. Her esophagus closed up somewhat so they had to open it up. There were many emergency trips like this. Usually it was around holiday times that things would start to really go bad and she would have to go to the hospital. Finally the doctor said there was nothing more to do. I still had the hope that she would make it. We called the funeral parlor and we made all the arrangements, but I still had hopes.

VERA AND NANCY

Even in the face of imminent death, Anna Marie could not believe that Caroline would die. Vera, likewise, shared her sense of shock and disbelief. Vera's partner was diagnosed with ovarian cancer and underwent surgery followed by months of chemotherapy. Vera explained how they met and what their relationship was like before Nancy became ill:

My partner's name was Nancy. We met almost seventeen years ago. Nancy was just being kicked out of a relationship at that point and I was just coming out of a marriage of fifteen years. I had known that I was a lesbian almost the entire time I was married, but I was afraid to live on my own so I stayed married for quite a long time. I had met Nancy before, but nothing sort of clicked between us until right after I left my husband. Nancy and I drove together to a dance and this time I was besotted with her. I was just completely enamored of her.

We had our first date shortly after that, but we had a really rocky first year because Nancy was just coming out of this other relationship and was determined not to get into anything too soon. I, on the other hand, was ready to settle down immediately. So it was a rocky first year, but we both hung in there, through a variety of difficult circumstances. We actually moved in together after we had been together about maybe a year and a half, although in reality we were living together much sooner than that.

After we had been together for about two and a half years, we had a commitment ceremony, which was totally fun. We just loved every minute of the planning. A lot of our lesbian friends were not very supportive. The most supportive people in our lives, unfortunately, were our straight friends, but we had a fabulous time. And once we got past the first hard year, we were both completely devoted to each other and to the relationship. And that never wavered.

We hung in there through some really hard times. I am an incest survivor and I had about four years of really doing a lot of very intense incest work, and I always said it was really Nancy's stick-to-it-ness and patience and sense of humor that got us through that one. And we just loved each other so much.

We were very, very different from each other in almost every way you can think of. I come from a liberal, Democratic family, and I am Jewish. Nancy came from a conservative Republican and Methodist upbringing and just everything about us was very different. We used to joke that our taste in women was opposite and our taste in movies and things like that. But we just liked each other so much, and respected each other so much, that our differences just were not issues. We were able to just sort of lovingly laugh at the differences. I am not saying that we were perfect by any means, but we just did differences really well.

We were both out to our families. We were both out in almost all aspects of our lives. Nancy taught people who were blind and visually impaired to use canes and take buses and stuff like that. She came out fifteen years before I did. She was out at work, she was out to all her friends, and she was out to her family. When I came out, I came out to my family and all of my friends. I am a faculty member at a state university. I do not come out to my classes, but I am out everywhere else on campus.

It is really hard for me to imagine what it would have been like to be in a relationship, let alone in a relationship where someone subsequently got sick, without being out. I would think that burden would be almost unbearable.

Then came Nancy's diagnosis.

We celebrated Christmas that year and Nancy was still feeling pretty good except for being very tired. Then in January, she woke up in the middle of the night having trouble breathing, and we went to the emergency room. It turned out that it was her kidneys that were causing her problems, so she had dialysis twice. You know, in retrospect, I should have realized she was dying, but I just could not.

JOY AND BARBARA

In Vera's story we again hear the denial of a partner dying. It was just too hard to face, so we focused on any little hint of progress, any sign of recovery instead. Joy also kept assuming Barbara would get better, but Barbara hid the seriousness of her illness from Joy. After Barbara's death, Joy felt not only bereft but also betrayed. Barbara and Joy had met at a Golden Threads Celebration in Provincetown, Massachusetts. Barbara lived in New Zealand and Joy lived in Germany. Joy shared how different their backgrounds were:

She had been born in the West End of London, watched her second grade best friend killed in a German bombing, was nurtured away from stuttering by a loving father, had a Cockney accent during her growing years, hated her mother, and knew she was a lesbian at a very young age. She did the bar scene, made love to women continuously (a real womanizer), had a marvelous sense of humor, and, with the encouragement of her father, she studied hard and became an accountant.

I, on the other hand, was reared in a sweet little town south of Chicago, religious by choice, never entered a bar until years later, studied classical piano throughout my childhood, attended college and university, taught in the NYC public school system for four years, and then started teaching in Germany for children of the U.S. military.

Despite such different backgrounds, they met one year at the hotel where the Golden Threads Celebration was held in Provincetown. Joy described the moment she first saw Barbara.

> I looked at her and saw a gorgeously dressed woman: suit, nylons, heels, perfect makeup and hairstyle. She was slim, hazel-eyed and spoke the Queen's English. *What's a straight woman like her doing here?* I wondered.

Joy was embarrassed when she realized later that Barbara was indeed a lesbian.

> Barbara pursued me carefully and politely with marvelous humor during the following week. I did not realize she was pursuing me since my nature is always to make friends, plus I could never dream that such a woman of her countenance could ever be interested in me for more than an acquaintanceship.

After meeting, Barbara was able to spend periods of time with Joy in Germany. She arrived on one such visit with what she told Joy was a cold. Despite Joy's loving care, she did not get better.

> I had to put her back on the plane after two weeks, and she returned to her doctor in England (where her family lived). I was worried. Finally she said she felt a bit better, and was flying to me for a special talk. I picked her up from the airport and brought her home once again.
>
> She told me that she had discussed the problem with the doctor and that the wet, cold weather in Germany was not helping her situation. She stated to the doctor that it was summer in New Zealand and the weather was hot and that she could better recuperate there. He agreed. Once she was in New Zealand, I was on the phone to ask how she was progressing. It was *then* that she finally broke down and announced that she had lung cancer and it was inoperable. I broke down on the phone crying and could not regain my composure. She said to hang up and she would phone back a bit later.

Step by step she got worse, but I did not really know it was going to mean death because Barbara let me expound on the fact that John Wayne had a cancerous lung removed and lived, plus the fact that I had just learned that the bark of the juniper tree might be good for treating lung cancer. She always behaved in a manner that indicated to me that these things could truly help her.

In April, Barbara phoned me to say that she was going to hospital for a few days for special tests and that she would phone me from there. I learned several frantic weeks later she had died in the hospital! Barbara did not want the burden of her cancer on me and was polite and loving on the phone calls, but she withheld the preciousness needed between two loving partners of being together.

Anger about our partner's death is one of the emotions we experience as we grieve, but the sense of betrayal that Joy felt because Barbara was not honest with her intensified Joy's pain even more. Although Barbara was sick over a period of time, Joy experienced her unanticipated death as a complete shock.

TRACI AND DANA

When Traci shared her story with me, she told me how happy she and Dana were before Dana became sick:

Dana and I had our future planned—we were "in love," and loved each other. Being lesbians for many years, we knew what we wanted—we knew this was "it"! We bought a condominium that was situated on a lake. We had everything we wanted—each other.

Our lives were very full. We had a huge lesbian community of friends. We attended parties every weekend, and still had time by ourselves. Life was great! We had future plans of retiring in Florida. We loved outdoor activities and warm weather.

Dana and I were "out" in our condominium. Our neighbors all knew our lifestyle but did not question us about it. It was just accepted. We lived our lives like everyone else in our neighborhood. However, I could not be out at my job—I am an elementary school teacher. I could be fired if it was known that I was a lesbian!

A lump in Dana's neck was diagnosed as lung cancer, and Traci shared their reactions.

> We were scared and devastated. Watching Dana fail quickly from both the cancer and the chemotherapy was horrible. The cancer quickly spread. Hospice was now in our lives. Life as we knew it was over.

Yes, life as we knew it was over. From the moment our partner was diagnosed or from the moment she suddenly passed away, life as we had known it would never be the same again.

MARILYN AND CHERYL

It was Marilyn's partner's reaction of denial that Marilyn described rather than her own. Cheryl lived her last months in denial of her approaching death, much as she and Marilyn had lived in denial of their lesbian relationship for thirty-one years. Marilyn explained,

> After a year of fighting our passion, agonizing over its morality, getting caught making out in a car and threatened by the police, we made the decision to pledge our lives to one another, even if it was only in the privacy of our own home, and to adopt two disabled children. We are talking the 1970s then, so the adoptions were as two single friends who were doing something altruistic.
>
> We lived a very conservative life and were totally in the closet. We had no contact with the gay community and in actuality could probably have been considered homophobic. We were none of the stereotypes; we were just us. We purchased a home together, adopted the two children (later a third) we wanted, and did everything together. We taught in the same school, commuted to work together. Our social lives revolved around the kids and the extensive volunteering that we did in the handicapped community. Everybody thought we were wonderful, giving ladies. No one spoke the "L" word. We planned to continue exactly as we were and retire sometime in our sixties.

But then Cheryl was diagnosed with ALS (amyotrophic lateral sclerosis), Lou Gehrig's disease.

The last normal day of our lives came in June 1998. Cheryl went to the orthopedist for a cortisone shot since she was experiencing some trouble with her knee. It was an on-and-off-again condition that she had been treated for before. The orthopedist was concerned about what he said were some subtle signs of some type of nerve problem that he observed in her leg and sent her for an EMG (electromyogram). We were too busy to be bothered, but about a month later our youngest son was having surgery and we managed to squeeze in the test for Cheryl.

To our horror, the radiologist told her he saw signs of a neurodegenerative disease such as ALS. He should never have just told her like that alone. It was news that would have been better broken together with the neurologist or orthopedist. We had an appointment with a neurologist within two days who said that her symptoms did not match the usual course for ALS, although he would not rule it out. He sent us to a research specialist in New York for further evaluation.

Meanwhile, we were following up on the possibility that this was late-stage Lyme disease as we lived in the woods and were campers, and not everyone with Lyme has the bull's-eye rash pattern. We were terrified and spent the hours that were not filled with normal routines and work crying and searching the Internet for information. We told the doctors that we were sisters.

The results came back by mail that Cheryl had bulbar-onset ALS. It is the less common and faster-progressing form of the illness. For about a year she had been treated by the allergist and ear, nose, and throat doctor for asthma and vocal cord abuse, caused, we thought, by the strain on her voice from shouting as a coach and using her voice all day teaching and parenting. No one had a suspicion that these were actually the early symptoms of ALS because she was not showing any motor signs.

Cheryl went into denial. She was not going to die and we would not discuss it. She would not go back to the doctor. After all, he had offered no hope.

While researching what could be done to treat ALS, Cheryl found a lump in her breast that was diagnosed as breast cancer.

At least this was something we could fight! The surgeon was wonderful and compassionate. Within a week and a half she had a lumpectomy. Healing was very slow, probably due to the ALS. I remember one terrifying incident when we were at home and Cheryl started screaming from the bathtub. Blood was spurting from the wound site all the way onto the walls. There was an infection and it had split open the surgery site. I stopped the bleeding and called the doctor and did as he instructed.

Our next two months were spent on daily radiation. Meanwhile both of us were still teaching and Cheryl was still driving. Her voice became worse and as radiation progressed she became weaker but she would not take a leave of absence. Just before Thanksgiving she had the vocal cord implant surgery and it did help a bit with volume and clarity.

Christmas was bittersweet that year while we wondered how many more we would have together. Would a cure be found? The research sounded so promising. Two days after Christmas there was another setback: a blood clot that clogged the artery from the ankle to the groin. I saw it in the morning and knew at once what it was. She was in the hospital within hours. They had a terrible time with the IVs. Her veins kept collapsing. Her circulation was bad from the ALS and worse on the side where the cancer had been.

It was a nightmare, and she was a terrible and terrified patient. In April, at the administration's insistence, Cheryl finally took a medical leave of absence. She would not retire because she held onto the hope that a cure would happen.

We had been given a glimmer of hope due to the fact that the cancer and ALS had been diagnosed within a month of each other. There was a possibility that this was a rare autoimmune response by the body to the cancer cells gone haywire and not truly ALS. Now our problem was that the treatment could not be done while she was on blood thinners. To prevent the reoccurrence of life-threatening blood clots forming, she had to be on a blood thinner for six months. So we waited but she got progressively worse.

She was so afraid yet so brave. The final test results showed that the two conditions (ALS and cancer) were just coincidental. For the ALS, there was nothing that could be done other than to arrange for physical and occupational therapy, which Cheryl refused. Since the bulbar form of ALS initially attacks the swallowing and speech areas, eating became harder and harder. Speech became impossible to be understood by anyone but me.

Throughout it all, I was the sole caregiver. Cheryl would not let me bring in any help. I was her total support. Sometimes she seemed to be irrational. She became skeletal and still refused to let anyone but me help her. Meanwhile I was supporting the kids and seeing they got to their programs and appointments.

Finally I called hospice. Mainly they were there for me. I needed medical information. I needed to know what to expect and I needed someone to talk to. Cheryl was not cooperative. In the beginning a nurse came once or twice a week to check her vitals, but I still did all of the caregiving. At least she finally gave in to having a hospital bed downstairs and a commode. That, combined with the lift chair and wheelchair we already had, made it a little easier to care for her.

As the days wore on she became weaker. She slept more often. She was not in physical pain, but she was in emotional agony. The hospice doctor prescribed medication to relieve some of the anxiety. In mid-March, the hospice nurse sat down with me and explained the physiological process of dying. I was given an emergency kit with instructions of who to call and what to do if Cheryl became very agitated or had trouble breathing. She told me it would not be long now. I knew that. Cheryl was starving to death slowly, minute by minute. The last week her pulse was weak and erratic. She was consuming almost no liquids and was awake only for short periods of time. But the kids had sports things going on and she wanted to be there for them, so she willed herself to live. Even the morning of the day she died, she told me "No," she was not leaving us.

Cheryl and I never discussed her funeral. She would not discuss dying, so how could we discuss a funeral? She was too afraid and in denial.

Cheryl's denial was a barrier that prohibited her and Marilyn from talking about what was happening and saying good-bye to each other.

SAMANTHA AND MARIE

Samantha's partner also denied that she was dying until right at the end. Samantha and Marie met at a lesbian bar. Samantha was recovering from a broken heart and not interested in getting involved with someone new. Marie, on the other hand, was eager to be in a relationship. Samantha explained,

> Over the course of the next year I watched Marie go through a lot of changes. She was from Peru and felt a little rootless and crazy after splitting from her American husband. I thought that she needed to go through some of that craziness. When she started to calm down and I had observed her for a year, I realized how intelligent and kind she could be. She became more beautiful to me instead of less for getting to know her. It was then that I approached her and asked if she would like to get together and try to make it work. I promised her that I would put everything I had into the relationship if she would give it a try. She agreed and we got together. She was twenty-nine and I was thirty-seven.

At the time, Samantha was a professional firefighter, and Marie was in graduate school. Samantha accompanied Marie on the day she became a U.S. citizen and had this to say about her:

> Marie was very into anything American and loved to throw barbecues, which we did frequently. Marie was a vivacious woman that everyone loved and, even though I was a Leo, I didn't mind letting her bask in the spotlight because she was such a pleasure to watch. She was funny and silly and serious and extremely intuitive when you could pin her down. She was a lot of fun to be with.
>
> We also fought a lot and she fought passionately; it was part of her cultural background. But even then I knew that she loved me, which enabled me to love her back just as much. We planned that, when she finished her PhD, we would move to wherever she got the high-dollar job and then I would go back to art school. So many plans and dreams we had together.

One day Marie felt a lump in her armpit. She had poison ivy on her wrist so she and Samantha both thought that maybe the lump was just a swollen lymph node because of the poison ivy. Samantha related what happened next:

> Normally I went to doctor appointments with her because she didn't like to go alone. I went to the initial appointment with her and they did a needle biopsy on the lump. I was working a twenty-four-hour shift at the fire department when she went for the results. I hated that I could not go with her because I knew how she was and we were a little concerned that they had wanted to do a needle biopsy.
>
> I was at work when Marie showed up there. She asked to talk to me so I went outside, where she broke down crying and said that she had cancer. I was devastated. I went numb. Later I broke down and started crying in front of my captain and asked if I could go home. Somehow it sounded and felt like a death sentence.
>
> For me, that was when hell started. Marie immediately began very aggressive chemotherapy. She went into early menopause and lost all interest in sex, could not have an orgasm even if she tried, something that for Marie had always been easy. She lost her beautiful thick brown hair and she lost her energy. I went to every doctor appointment with her, taking notes and asking questions.
>
> Marie's parents flew in from Peru less than two days after we had the results, no permission asked. They had to be told the nature of our relationship before we went further. They were accepting of me because they had no choice. Marie and I did not get the time to process together at all.
>
> Three months earlier Marie had insisted that we get a puppy as practice for having a baby. We planned to ask my brother to donate sperm when we were both more settled. So I had a puppy to take care of, and Marie's parents, who did not speak any English, to house and feed. I was trying to do emergency rescue work but was having a harder and harder time distancing myself from the work. I ended up quitting my job at the fire department and working at a natural foods warehouse.
>
> After a month, Marie's father had to return to Peru and her mother stayed for a while longer. She was clearly at a loss and

unhappy being here. I could not talk to her, and Marie did not have the strength. It was a relief when she decided that it was time for her to go home. The house became a revolving door for friends and well-wishers to stop by and see Marie. She welcomed the attention, but I found it exhausting. After the chemo, Marie had both breasts removed and found that they were cancer free. We had hopes for a future.

Exactly a year later, however, Marie began having headaches and was unsteady on her feet. An MRI (magnetic resonance imaging) showed four brain tumors. Even then Marie fought to live.

Marie knew at that point that time was short. She did a lot of research on the computer and decided that her odds were better for a few extra months of life if she had brain surgery on the largest of the masses. She was adamant and I supported any and all decisions she made.

Once again Marie's parents came and stayed with us in our new home, which was only a little larger than the last. It was another uncomfortable month, only this time there was less hope. Thankfully they did not stay as long and went back home after the surgery with the promise to pay for both of us to fly to Peru when Marie got better. We had paid their plane fare and I was basically supporting their stay with us both times they came. I did not make very much money and normally we led a frugal existence, so this was stressing my resources heavily.

I went out with her and her best friend and we talked about the possibility of Marie dying. I told Marie that I wanted her to share with me what was going on with her and how she was feeling about it. She said that she would not, that it was personal and that it was none of my business. She rarely cried and she rarely let on that she was bothered by what was happening. That made it difficult for me to express my feelings so I, as a person, an individual with my own needs, hopes, and desires, shut down. Everything I did and thought about became for and about Marie. I ceased to exist. Marie had shut me out and I thought that she had every right to respond and act any way she damn well pleased. I could not possibly know what she was going through and I did not try to. I just tried to accept her mood swings, love her as much as she would let me, and feel as safe and loved as I could. Marie had the operation on her head and then they wanted to do what they called whole-brain radiation . . . basically cooking what was left of her brain. I was still trying to maintain the house, go to all of the appointments, give Marie anything and everything she wanted or needed, work, and take care of what was increasingly my only personal support, the dog.

The doctor put Marie on such a high dose of steroids that she was unable to sleep for the last two months. I would come out from the bedroom and find her sitting up with her computer still on in her lap, asleep. The steroids affected her so strongly that she became what I jokingly called "the grand dictatress." Her best friend even gave her a pillow that said "It's good to be Queen," so I was not the only one who noticed the change in her behavior.

I loved her so much and she was so driven not to accept what was going on that she became obsessive about the computer. A couple of weeks before Marie died, I realized that I was in way over my head trying to deal with what was going on by myself and in desperation I called my mother and she flew down to help me out. She was able to walk the dog and take care of the house while I took Marie to the hospital and continued to work. She went home a few days before Christmas. I stopped working when Marie started falling down and I realized that I was the only one who could pick her up.

Samantha wrote about a tender moment that she and Marie shared a few days before Marie died. Up until then, Marie had refused to talk about dying, but that night they took a shower together.

While we were in there, she asked me if I thought that we would ever make love again. I said "No" and we cried together in the shower and lovingly I bathed her. I will always be thankful for that. It was one of the few times that I felt we really connected and were able to express some of the pain and deep love that we had for one another.

The shock and then denial experienced by the women in this chapter, and in some cases their partner's denial, cushioned them from the full impact of what was happening. In essence, though, the soon-to-be-widows accompanied their dying partner on her journey to death at the same time that they themselves embarked on their own journey of grief.

Chapter 4

Long-Term Illness

Although fourteen of the widows in this book dealt with the shock of having their life partner diagnosed with a terminal illness, five others became involved with women who already had health problems. None of these five, however, realized how quickly death would come.

HEATHER AND RUTH

Heather fell in love with Ruth, knowing up front that Ruth was in poor health. She decided that she needed to follow her heart.

I met Ruth when we worked on a lesbian hotline together. I was twenty-two, a senior in college, and she was thirty-one, already on disability from diabetes. I knew I liked her—she was funny, smart, . . . okay, and cute. I brought my newly adopted kitten to the hotline office just to see her face light up.

I knew from the start that I would lose her. She had had diabetes since infancy, and it had taken its toll. She had lost almost all her vision, as well as her left leg below the knee, and at least one toe on the other foot. She had a wonderful sense of humor, and the most beautiful blue eyes that were so expressive you could swear she could see out of them. I can't tell you why I fell for a sick, disabled woman. Perhaps on some level I was afraid of a long-term commitment, but most of it was simply that I was very much in love with her.

Her friends disapproved, of course. A twenty-two-year-old baby dyke would only break her heart. Her last girlfriend was older than her, and still bailed soon after Ruth got sick in the middle of one night. It took about a year, but friends gradually realized I was planning to stick around. Ruth probably always knew that. So did I.

When I think about what our relationship was like, I divide it roughly down the middle into two stages. The first was wonderful, although still full of medical crises. We had lots of energy for each other, and relished one another's company. I best remember the little things. Lying in bed together, hearing the sound of the geese at the pond nearby followed by Ruth's predictable, "Honey, your ride's here." The sun shining in her hair as I rounded the corner to pick her up, able to watch her for a while before she knew I was approaching. Lots of time with me reading to her. The stories of when she was a teacher and got in trouble with her principal for having the kids sing "This Land Is Your Land" instead of the national anthem.

We talked about having a commitment ceremony. We were just starting to hear of women doing that, and one couple we knew had a ceremony to celebrate ten years together and to reaffirm their commitment to one another. But we didn't know what we wanted the ceremony to look like, and never got beyond talking. We gave up on the idea and went shopping for rings together, later putting them on one another's fingers and agreeing to stay together for life.

Heather felt it was important to talk about what it was like to take care of someone with a disability and how Ruth's friends shared in that care.

She had a very strong group of friends, and their support allowed her to live independently. Gradually she and her friends taught me what I needed to know to help her and deal with medical emergencies, and we all relaxed into our daily routines. Her morning routine was to wheel her chair down the long hallway, with her cat Boo standing on her lap—Ruth always called Boo her hood ornament.

Your study isn't on coping with illness and disability, but it is hard to talk about her impending death without at least giving you a picture of these. One of the complications of her diabetes was neurological damage. This manifested itself several ways, but two were most notable: She could no longer sense when her blood sugar was dipping too low, and her digestive system often went on strike, leaving food to sit in her stomach undigested, or to come back up. The combination of these, as you might imagine, was a doozy, and she had frequent and severe insulin (low blood sugar) reactions. So emergencies were a way of life for all of us. Her friends and I had a structured system of checking on her regularly; she had to answer the phone or face a visit from one of us or the paramedics.

Later on, things got much harder. She began to devote more and more of her energy to just managing the basics. We stopped having sex. We stopped having stimulating discussions. We continued loving each other deeply, but I lost the feeling of a mutual adult relationship. I suspect the repeated insulin reactions (hundreds over a few years) caused some minimal brain damage. I loved her still, but she was not the Ruth I had fallen in love with a few short years earlier.

I requested nonmonogamy. She agreed, I now believe, only because she did not feel as though she had any choice in the matter. Our relationship gradually shifted. I continued to feel a lifetime commitment to her, but was also moving on. If I were straight, and married, I would have said that we were separated, but with no intention of getting a divorce. I longed for a way to talk about our relationship. Sometimes I called her my lover, sometimes my ex. Neither fit. She was my partner.

Twelve years ago she had an appointment with her social worker. That day at noon, a friend was scheduled to check on her. This friend often forgot the noon call, but remembered that day. Ruth was okay, but tired. About to have a nap—she loved her naps. She did not wake up from that one. She was forty years old.

DALE AND CAROL

Heather's story is an example of how a community of women rallied to make Ruth's quality of life the best possible. Dale, on the other hand, was Carol's sole support until Carol had to be placed in a nursing home. Dale assumed the caretaker role for much longer than any of the other widows who sent me their stories.

Dale and Carol met at a New Moon gathering when Dale was still married and had three young children. Carol waited for and emotionally supported Dale through the divorce process, agreeing to keep their relationship a secret so that Dale would not lose custody of her children. Dale described Carol as one of the most incredible women she had ever known.

> She was so kind and she knew how to listen. She was a full professor and she talked me into going back to school to get my master's in teaching. I never felt like I was much of a student, but she convinced me I could do it and she would help me. She was so patient through it all.

Carol had been diagnosed with MS (multiple sclerosis) five years prior to their meeting, but she showed no symptoms of the disease other than tiring easily. Gradually, however, she experienced "episodes" and each time would lose a little more of her functioning.

> It is difficult to describe the progression because it was a slow gradual thing, and we just dealt with the problems as they came up. I went to the doctors with her and gave the IVs when it came time to do that. I would often carry her into the house when she just was too tired to get her legs to move. I have to say, though, that throughout the whole time, she was always positive and upbeat.
>
> Right after we bought a house, she had a major exacerbation and went into rehab, which helped for a little while. When she was in rehab, her father died. They let her go to his funeral but had refused to let her out to see him before he died. Sometimes the medical establishment really makes me angry. At that time I did not have enough self-confidence to say "Screw you!" to the hospital. They made a bad situation worse.

Carol's health slowly deteriorated until Dale had to place her in a nursing home.

> I hurt my back at work and asked her sister if she could take Carol for a while. She refused. I had to find someone to come in and lift her to bed every night. It was at this point that I felt like I was sinking. Carol went into the nursing home in May of 1992 and I have carried the guilt of that with me ever since. We had been together seven years.

Carol lived another seven years in the nursing home, dying in Dale's arms at age sixty-one. About those seven years Dale wrote,

> I used to go by the nursing home on my way into work in the morning. Then I started working a second job and I would go into the nursing home to tuck her in at night. If she was sick, I would go in during my lunch. I can't even begin to recount the battles at the nursing home. They are amazing places and you really have to stand your ground; otherwise they just try and take over making all the decisions whether or not you want them to.
>
> I had to get into a yelling match once because they brought in some outside psychiatrist and did not tell me they were doing this. They had no excuse. I was in every day. I also had medical durable power of attorney. There was a time when I went in when they had not fed her; many times when they had not bathed her. I kept a close eye on her skin and she still ended up with occasional bedsores. This went on for seven years. It was difficult watching her fade away by inches.

Despite the tremendous toll that caregiving took on her life, Dale wrote, "All total we had fourteen years together, and I would not trade one minute of it for anything in the world. I was so lucky having her in my life for all too brief a time."

PAM AND SANDY

Carol did not appear to be ill when she and Dale met. Neither did Sandy, who was in remission from breast cancer when Pam met her. Pam explained,

> Breast cancer is rampant throughout Sandy's family. Her mother died of it when she was forty-eight. Sandy and her twin sister were sixteen at the time. Several of Sandy's aunts and first cousins have had breast cancer and were successfully treated. Sandy was first diagnosed with breast cancer when she was forty.

Pam knew that Sandy had been diagnosed with breast cancer years before they met, but the doctor told Sandy that surgery had removed all signs of the cancer.

My lover Sandy and I were together for a little over ten years before she died of breast cancer. We had actually met about three years before we got together at an AIDS training retreat for new volunteers. Sandy was with another woman at that time, but I was intrigued that I was not the only Jewish lesbian in the world. Sandy and I stayed in touch over the years, and then she and Casey broke up.

I asked Sandy to accompany me to a wedding in P'Town and she said yes. We became lovers there. I was thirty and she was forty-eight. We came home and, while I held on to my apartment for several months, for all intents and purposes, I was living with her. So, I moved in with my Yorkshire terrier, Boo.

Sandy was a psychotherapist in private practice and was practicing out of her house. So, she and Boo saw clients all day until I came home from work and then Boo would come downstairs to see me. I am a photographer, and at the time I was working at a commercial photo lab as a customer service rep.

From the very beginning, it did not feel like a "new" relationship. We both felt that we had been together forever. Not that we did not have problems, but there was something so special about our being together. I told Sandy that I would give our relationship thirty years and then reevaluate. It was our special joke.

Sandy had three adult children. One lived here nearby and had two children, a son, age sixteen, and a daughter, fourteen. Another daughter was married and lived in another part of the state; she had two boys, ages eight and six. Sandy's son was married, and he and his wife were trying to have a baby. Our lives revolved around the children.

After being together for one year, Sandy and I had a commitment ceremony. We were surrounded by family (except for my family; I didn't invite them) and many friends. We were married under a chuppa, the Jewish wedding canopy that I made for us. A rabbi and cantor, both women, both dear friends of ours, performed the ceremony. We were also very involved with our local gay and lesbian Jewish groups.

Sandy's health seemed fine when we met, despite her having been treated for breast cancer years before, but then she began not to feel well. She had exploratory surgery to see why her lungs were filling with liquid. While Sandy was in recovery, the doctor told me that inside her chest were about one hundred tumors shaped like bunches of grapes. He did a biopsy and it was indeed cancer, the same breast cancer that had been surgically cured all those years earlier.

She underwent chemo. I think it was six or eight rounds. I did my best to comfort and entertain her, along with many, many friends and family. Both her sisters came a number of times. After about the fourth or fifth treatment, her hair fell out while I was helping her shower. She was devastated. But, after recovering for a few days at home after each treatment, she went back to work. She tried wigs and different hats but finally settled on a green baseball cap.

She was seen regularly by our internist who, God bless him, was the perfect Jewish mother. The oncologist was as perfect a doctor as anyone could hope to have. Blood work, chest X-rays, and various scans showed all to be well for a while. Then Sandy found a lump in her other breast. It was cancer and she had another mastectomy. More chemo and radiation but after several months it was clear that the treatment was not working. The oncologist told us that there was nothing else he could do.

We arranged for in-home hospice care. The aide, Mary, helped Sandy bathe, dress, and eat; she also changed the bed linens and did the laundry. The nurses came every couple of days to monitor her condition. At the same time, my mother had been diagnosed with lung cancer and then had two strokes. She and my father were living in Texas at the time. I needed to see my mother, so with Sandy's sister staying with her for the weekend, I flew to Texas. My mother was in intensive care when I got a call from our friend, Miriam. Sandy had fallen and it was clear that she was not going to be able to be cared for at home any longer. The doctor decided to admit Sandy to an inpatient hospice. I said good-bye to my mother and my brother and flew home as soon as I could.

Sandy was in hospice for two weeks. Someone was always there with her, and usually all day and well into the evening, people would come and visit. I was always treated with incredible kindness and respect by the staff at the hospice. I was given complete access at all times. Three days before she died, she became comatose.

The folks at hospice were so wonderful with her. They attended to every possible need. Hospice folks are the most incredibly awesome people I know. I have the greatest respect for the work they do. It is mentally and physically exhausting, but they were always available.

MAUREEN AND ROBIN

Similar to Pam, Maureen also began a relationship with a woman who was in remission from breast cancer. Robin and Maureen met when they worked at the same hospital. They began dating after Robin left a note on Maureen's car, inviting her to her birthday party. When Maureen arrived, she discovered there was no party; she and Robin had a romantic evening together instead. Even though Maureen was twenty years younger than Robin, Maureen said it seemed like they were the perfect match. After about a year, they moved in together and Robin was supportive of Maureen's decision to become pregnant. Robin had battled breast cancer five years previously and went for regular six-month checkups.

> We met while she was in remission. She told me there was the risk of it coming back and that she could not guarantee that she would not get sick again. Somehow that seemed so unreal and far from my mind that I never thought it could actually happen. After I became pregnant, she went to the doctor for her routine six-month checkup, and, just like every six-month appointment, we just knew everything was okay. Well, not this time.
>
> The doctor found a swollen nodule in her neck that turned out to be cancerous. She had scans to see where the cancer had returned. It was found in her liver. She started going to chemo again. By then I was working at a different hospital than where her treatment was, so every Tuesday I took the afternoon off so I could be there for her. She never really complained about the pain or the chemo but you could see every week she got weaker and looked so tired all the time.

The early months of Maureen's pregnancy were filled with hospital and doctor visits for Robin, but Maureen never gave a thought to the idea that Robin might not survive. Maureen continued their story:

One day she fell out of the bed while trying to get to the bathroom in the middle of the night. When she fell, she broke her hip. She still managed to get around with the use of a walker and made it to work most days. She worked as the administrative assistant for the chief of pediatric surgery. She got so much support from her co-workers. They donated sick time for her to still get paid while going through chemo and did whatever they could to help. This helped so much because she felt needed and like she was still doing something. She really thought she would eventually go back to work full-time.

In the middle of the night one night, however, Robin woke Maureen up and said she needed to get to the hospital.

We gathered some stuff and got her to the emergency room. I thought this was going to be another visit to the ER, and we would be home again in a day or two. We were there about an hour or two when they asked if I was ready to sign the "Do Not Resuscitate" order. This was the first time I realized how bad Robin really was.

ROSE AND STEPH

Pam and Maureen began relationships with women who appeared to be healthy but were in remission from breast cancer, which then returned. Rose began a relationship with a woman who also appeared to be healthy even though she had a heart condition. Rose is a psychologist. She met Steph when they were both promoted to program coordinator at the hospital where they were employed. Rose's husband was also employed there. Rose wrote that, as they sat in weekly meetings together, her friendship with and admiration for Steph grew.

In the spring of 1990, I was flabbergasted one day to get a note from Steph (she was a prolific writer) professing her feelings for me. I had been aware of being attracted to women since early adolescence, but had never acted on that attraction, nor admitted it to anyone. That's another whole story.

I was then almost thirty-nine years old. I cannot begin to describe my agitation upon receiving that note! I was terrified. I was excited. I did not know what to do. Over time, I had become increasingly unhappy in my marriage as I realized that I wanted to be with a woman. I loved my husband, but he was simply the wrong gender. But what if I was wrong? What if being with a woman was not really what I wanted either? After all, I had never actually tried that. I was a mess!

I knew I did not want her to just go away so I wrote back, confirming that I was attracted to her but reminding her of my marriage. She began courting me. She was nothing if not romantic. Within a month or two, I knew that I had to take the risk of upsetting my entire life to be with her.

Eventually Rose divorced her husband and Steph moved in with her.

Our life together was a mixed bag. At first we were giddy with excitement. I was busy learning about the world of lesbians and gay men. Steph delighted in teaching me everything she knew, and I was an eager pupil. We settled into a fairly routine domestic life, working and maintaining a home, socializing with other gays and lesbians in the bars. We planned to grow old together.

Shortly thereafter, however, Steph was forced to quit work for health reasons.

She had had two heart attacks in her early thirties before I knew her. This was the first real test of our relationship. Neither of us realized how much of our identities we derived from our careers, and she was lost without the structure, status, and income from a full-time job. Fortunately, her job provided a moderate amount of disability pay, so we were not completely reliant on my income alone. Eventually she qualified for Social Security disability payments.

At times it was hard to believe that she was sick. She looked healthy, and much of the time she was. But any time she had a relapse, she was very, very ill, requiring at least a week of hospitalization each time. I am not sure that there was ever an exact diagnosis of what was wrong with her. Essentially, her blood tended to clot for unknown reasons, which would lead to problems with her already damaged heart. One hospitalization was specifically for congestive heart failure.

Compounding her medical picture was the fact that she was an alcoholic. Our physician was aware of this, but probably seriously underestimated its impact on Steph's health. I know that *I* certainly minimized her drinking, having never been in close contact with an alcoholic before this. Because so much of the gay community in which we were involved centered on the bars, I did not really think about the fact that she was drinking much of the time. And for quite some time, I did not know that she had begun drinking during the day at home. She referred to herself as a "functional alcoholic," and she could indeed drink a great deal with no apparent effect (until she passed out). To this day, the memory of that astounds me.

Rose reported that she and Steph slowly began to have problems in their relationship.

Many of our problems revolved around the fact that I had to get up in the morning and work all day. I usually wanted to stay home in the evenings, while she wanted us to go to the bar, staying until it closed. Much as I enjoyed the socializing, I could not take the hours.

Steph was lost without the structure and identity provided by a career, and her drinking increased. Her best male friend died of AIDS, leaving her even more bereft. As appalled as I am now to consider the timing, we split up shortly after his death. I cannot remember the exact pretense for our split, only that I had given her an ultimatum and she crossed over my "line in the sand." I do remember that we took pains to let people know that it was not because of her drinking. And I truly wanted to believe that, but, in hindsight, I know that the drinking really was at the core of our split.

At first Steph moved into a nearby apartment. They talked on the phone daily and saw each other several times a week. Then Steph moved to Florida to live with another woman, but Rose said that did not affect the sense of connection that they had. They continued to talk several hours a day, running up astronomical phone bills. One day Rose received a phone call from Steph's doctor.

She had developed a blood clot in her large intestine and they were going to have to operate immediately to remove part of her intestine. The surgeon did not think Steph would survive the surgery. I was stunned. I was devastated. Despite the saying, time does not heal all wounds because I still remember and feel how I felt at the moment I heard that news. The pain is still intense when I think about it. I think that was really the first time I fully understood that she could die.

Rose stayed with Steph for ten days, then returned home. Steph called her a few days later, saying that she was being rushed into surgery again. Their last words to each other were "I love you." Again, in Rose's story, you hear that sense of denial that we felt until something happened that forced us to face that our partner was dying. Even though Rose and Steph were not in a sexually intimate relationship at the time of Steph's death, Rose still experienced Steph's death as the loss of her soul mate.

NORA AND ANNE

Pam, Maureen, and Rose became involved with women who appeared to be healthy but who had health conditions that ended up taking their lives. Nora, on the other hand, knew that Anne was sick from lung cancer and that eventually she would lose her. They were close friends for about two years before they became lovers. Nora explained why she decided to go ahead and become involved with Anne even though she was ill:

> My friends, and even Anne, cautioned me against taking our friendship onto that different plane. They had watched me go through the death of my eldest son just twelve months before. I told them that if his death taught me anything, it was that life is too precious to waste a moment. There are no second chances.
> Anne and I lived by the corny old AA motto "One day at a time." We discovered a wonderful love that came as a total surprise to both of us. My friends still cautioned me but I told them, "If this did not feel so right, I would have every reason in the world to walk away." I suppose I foolishly believed that somehow our love could work miracles. People do survive cancer.

During the brief time that we were together, we found a wonderful balance between doing things as a family with our two children and doing things together as a couple. We also respected each other's space and times when we needed to be alone. Although we knew there could not be a far distant future, we talked about the life we could have together. We both loved the outdoors, horses, music, and books. One of the highlights of our short time together was a four-day trip to Sedona, Arizona, where Anne had spent time when she first qualified as a doctor.

Nora admitted, however, that she thought that they would have more than five months together.

I knew she had lung cancer when we became lovers, but I had no idea how little time she had left. When her health really began to fail and we knew the end would come soon, she asked me if I had any regrets. My immediate answer was to say, "None." Moments later I said, "No, I have two regrets. The first is that we did not meet earlier. The second is that we did not have more time."

Despite the pain of losing Anne, Nora had no regrets about their brief time together.

PAT AND BETTY

In contrast to the brief time Anne and Nora had, Pat had thirty-two years with Betty who, even at a young age, had medical problems. Pat and Betty met when they were in the army when both were in their twenties.

Betty had been on convalescent leave when I arrived and I had joined the WAC (Women's Army Corps) softball team in her absence. I was not universally welcomed into that group of mostly lesbians as I was engaged to be married to a man at the time. Fortunately that turned out to be "just a phase" and I got over it when Betty returned to post and fell in love with me at first sight.

This was the first lesbian sexual encounter for both of us. We decided right away that this was right for us. We exchanged rings and the vow "till death do us part." We were together for the next thirty-one years until Betty's death. Due to the time and place that we got together, pre-Stonewall and in the military, being out was not an option.

First Betty and then Pat left the army. Over the years they lived in different places and worked at various jobs. Pat explained how very different their backgrounds were:

>   Since college, I have always been "out" at my workplaces. Once I was out of the army and could be myself, I felt generally comfortable being out. For me, being lesbian is my natural state; no amount of socialization has overcome that feeling. Perhaps that is because I had no formal religious training in any church and there was no negative input from my family about lesbianism during my childhood. I always was confident that I could accomplish whatever I wanted to do. When I realized that I was a lesbian, it was just naming part of the package that is me, and it did not diminish my belief in myself.
>   Betty did not have this luxury. She grew up in a small city in upstate New York. Her father was a mill worker and they experienced extreme poverty. She was brought up in the Catholic Church and, although she did not attend after she was a teenager, she never forgot the humiliation she experienced in the church due to their poverty. Betty's mother and sister remain active in the church to this day, and for a long time they could not accept Betty's lesbianism.
>   There was a period of estrangement from Betty's family after her mother and sister read a letter that I had sent her when she was living with her mother and I was still in the army. Betty told her mother that she would have to choose—Betty as she was, with me, or no daughter. When it came down to her disappearing from their lives altogether or accepting her, they grudgingly accepted her lifestyle. This was very helpful for her brother when he finally came out to his mother. To this day, her love and devotion to me in the face of familial disapproval astonishes me, but I think that Betty was never really comfortable with herself as a lesbian. This led to much unhappiness and distress for her through the years.

Betty had many medical episodes throughout their years together. She had five surgeries in their first four years together. She later was diagnosed with a cancerous tumor in her right breast and had a modified radical mastectomy of the right breast. She also had left breast tissue removed because of pervasive fibrocystic disease. A few years later she had a hysterectomy.

In late 1989, it was discovered that her kidney function was only 50 percent. Through a controlled diet she was able to function quite well for a couple of years before it got much worse; she was able to put off dialysis until 1993. She received a transplant and enjoyed reasonably good health for quite a while. She participated in the 1994 and 1996 USA Transplant Games in tennis and the softball throw. She won the gold medal in her age group for the softball throw in 1996.

In 1997, she became violently ill and I had to take her to the emergency room. A CT (computerized tomography) scan revealed that there was at least one tumor in the liver. The oncologist told us that cancer in the liver gave Betty only months, not years, to live. Betty refused to accept that. She intended to fight it, and fight she did, right up until the end. She chose to undergo chemotherapy and continued with that course for the remaining twelve months of her life.

We had moved her mother to our home in March 1998. It was a fortunate thing, because Betty refused to have outside help. When she got bad, Mother stayed with her during the day while I was at work. They were able to talk and reminisce about their life; it was good for both of them. For me, it was not so good. Betty would not talk to me about the past, very little about the present, and absolutely nothing about the future during those last few months.

After her surgery in October, she went to the hospital almost monthly after chemo treatment because of diminished white cells. She spent Thanksgiving there. It was a horrible day for me because everyone came to my house, and I had to cook dinner for them, and then I took a meal for Betty and me to the hospital. The weight of what was happening got to me that day. I started crying as I realized and said aloud for the first time that Betty was dying.

What I did not know at the time was that my father was actually near death, having fallen and hit his head on a piece of furniture the day before. My sister did not tell me until after Betty had come home on Saturday. My father died early Sunday morning. I did not go back for the funeral because Betty's condition was so tenuous.

In April, I took Betty to the hospital for the last time. The tumor in the liver had grown so large that it had blocked the bile duct and she was severely jaundiced. She was extremely weak and was not eating or drinking very much. The liver function was diminishing significantly. She underwent a minor surgical procedure to insert a drainage tube in the liver to give her as much relief as possible. Up until that time her kidney had held up remarkably well, but as the liver failed, so did the kidney.

The doctor told me that now was the time to call anyone who needed to say good-bye. I called her mother, and she got in touch with Betty's brother and sister. Her brother came that afternoon and her sister came the next morning. She went into a coma and died about 1:45 a.m. Although she lived longer than her doctor anticipated, in the end, strong-willed though she was, she was unable to beat the odds.

When we cared for our loved one as she was dying, we experienced what grief counselors call anticipatory grief. That is, we began grieving before our partner actually died. Our challenge was to be present with our dying partner in the here and now while at the same time mourning the loss that we knew would come to us in the future. This was not easy to do.

For the lesbians whose stories are in this chapter, only one mentioned having trouble with medical doctors and facilities. The others were respected by the medical profession even though they were lesbians and not legally married. We will see in the upcoming chapters, however, how that was not always the case.

Chapter 5

The Caretaker Role

Emily spent six weeks in the hospital after her stomach surgery. She was home two weeks and then went back to the hospital for three more due to infection. After that, she made several short trips to the hospital for various procedures. At home, she slept in a hospital bed and required twenty-four-hour attendance. Most of the time she had to be fed through a feeding tube inserted into her abdomen. There were "leaks" and infections and medical procedures I had never heard of before, and I did things to take care of Emily that I never thought I would ever be willing to do. We scheduled family and friends to be with her during the day while I was at work, and a nurse's aide to be with her overnight so I could sleep. Caretaking filled my life when I was not working. When I reviewed my journal from that time, I noted that I wrote repeatedly about how exhausted I was.

I am so tired. I slept soundly for eight hours and I woke up feeling like I did not sleep at all. I have to leave shortly to teach but what I really want to do is crawl back into bed and sleep some more.

Mixed with the exhaustion and caretaking, however, was anger. Em was a really awful patient, demanding and impossible to please. I remember the day I came home from work to find her sitting up in bed, telling everyone in the room what she wanted them to do, and I thought to myself, *She looks like a queen on her throne ordering her subjects around.* I did not like that side of her at all!

The months from Emily's diagnosis until her death were a roller coaster of up-and-down emotions for both of us. There were days she wanted to live and days she wanted to die. She was delusional at times and would accuse me of things that were not true. For example, she would claim that I never visited her or that I refused to give her the scheduled medications. I knew these delusions were the result of the morphine she took for pain, but they were still hard to hear.

Sometimes we would have a good talk one day and she would not remember it the next. There were times we fought, times we talked lovingly, and times we cried together.

Friends told me repeatedly to take care of myself, but how do you take care of yourself when the person you love is dying? I would go back and forth between wanting to be with her every minute possible and wanting to run away. There were days that I wanted to escape from her neediness and other days that I did not want to leave her side, afraid to lose any moment we could have together.

As I stood at Em's bedside I realized: I have lost my best friend as well as my lover. I have no one to share my life with the way I shared it with Em. And whatever I got from being loved and listened to by her, I now have to find within myself. Her diagnosis has knocked the wind out of all of us.

I decided, after a couple of months of caretaking, that I needed more support than friends could give me, so I began seeing a therapist every other week. After hardly sleeping for the first couple of months, I also saw a doctor for medication. With my therapist, I talked about what was happening with Em, but mainly I dealt with guilt feelings, regrets, and anger about issues in our relationship. I was able to process the baggage between us so that I did not carry it with me after her death. One very helpful thing my counselor pointed out to me was that the anger and fighting we had experienced since Em's diagnosis were ways to divert us from grieving. It is easier to be angry than sad.

I kept working during those ten months that Emily was dying even though I felt guilty that I was not giving Em my undivided attention. I knew that I had to keep working in order to be able to support myself, but I think also that work was a therapeutic break for me from all the caregiving.

DONNA AND RANDI

Donna shared an interesting point of view about the dilemma of whether to keep working or not. First she related how she and Randi had met:

We met at the home of Randi's daughter-in-law, who was a musical colleague of mine for a number of years prior to her marriage. She had been trying all summer to introduce us because "I could see that they were part of the same thing." Randi and I immediately found common ground in an intense curiosity about one another. Here is another free-thinker who is about my size, has the same haircut as I do, is wearing the same color and style of clothing, has the same food preferences, has the same love of the outdoors and of traveling, lives with cats, has the same oddball sense of humor, always believed she would end up moving to California, has the same inordinately charming and disarming smile. Who is she? On our first camping trip two days later, we also discovered that we have the same birthday, twenty years apart. She was sixty-five and I was forty-five.

Randi introduced Donna to motorcycling. Although Donna had misgivings about Randi's safety on the motorcycle, it ended up being cancer, not motorcycling, that ended Randi's life. Donna wrote,

> I remember the day when I asked, "So, when do I get to see that motorcycle of yours?" She rode it to my house that night. It looked huge. She looked tiny sitting on it, disguised in her British waxed cotton riding suit, boots, helmet, gloves. I saw how happy it made her to ride, to own that fabulous bike, and I knew it would be easy to make room for a motorcyclist in my life.
>
> When we first became involved, I wondered what the chances were that she would die in a motorcycle accident. I saw that I would have to live with this possibility if I were to live with her. I knew that she would not stop riding, and I knew that if she died this way, she would have died doing what she loved most to do.
>
> My first teacher about grief was Randi. Throughout our relationship, she had been sparing with stories about her husband's death. The stories I heard most were the happy memories. But that changed when she knew she would die. She knew what I was going to experience, and so she told me of her husband's dying and of how she coped with it. When he became ill, she and her husband did not consider the possibility that he could actually die. Therefore, he made no will, and after his death, in the midst of her grief, she was faced with having the state take control of all the family assets and decide how to distribute them. She did not want that to ever happen to me.
>
> When we knew she was dying, my instinct was to spend every remaining moment with her, to cancel my appointments and

obligations and stay home. She told me that work had saved her after her husband's death. She advised that, if I did not *stop* doing my daily activities, then I would not be faced with having to *start* doing them again after her death. Immediately, I saw the wisdom in this, and so continued to work, making no new appointments, but keeping the ones already made.

Donna, like me, struggled with wanting to be with her partner and yet acknowledging that she needed to maintain her own life. Working full-time, caretaking when I was not working, and grieving over the loss I knew I would be facing left me feeling overwhelmed. In a dream I had, the image of a tidal wave expressed this feeling.

Dream: A huge tidal wave is coming, flooding the land. I stand still and wait for it, ride the heart of the wave as if I am walking on water, and come through unharmed. Later I realize I have lost my glasses but a young girl finds them in the basement. I am grateful. My interpretation: The water represents emotion. I am riding the wave of emotion of Em's illness and death. I will be able to ride it out okay and at the end gain some perspective.

A CHANGE OF ROLES

Rather than describing a sense of being overwhelmed, as I felt, Maureen described how her role changed when her partner was dying, from being Robin's lover to being her caregiver. When Robin was sent home from the hospital with instructions that she should be made comfortable, Maureen finally had to face reality.

I was totally devastated. I had no idea what to do. We had a new house, we had a baby on the way, and the love of my life was dying. Five days after we went to the emergency room, she was home and we were not partners or lovers anymore. Now I was her caretaker.

Yes, a caretaker. For those of us whose partner died from an illness rather than a sudden death, our roles changed as our partner first fought to live and then had to let go and die. In the last three months of Em's life, we went from one crisis to another, one hospital visit after another until, at the end, she was skin and bones, her skin yellowed with jaundice. During this time, Emily rewrote her will and planned her funeral. One month before she died, I wrote in my journal,

Em and I are talking every day now about her dying. I am grateful for this time, even though it is hard. I know in my heart that I just have to let her go and trust that there is some higher purpose in this that we just do not know. And trust that I will be okay even though I am terrified of living alone.

THE SUPPORT OF FRIENDS

By far the greatest blessing to me during the time that Emily was dying was the support of our wonderful friends. They not only supported me emotionally, they helped out in very physical, practical ways. One did our laundry, some brought meals, one took care of our household plants. Cards poured in. Friends and colleagues stopped by the house to pay their respects. One group of friends began meeting weekly in a healing prayer and drumming circle. One day a group of twenty-some women came to our home and sang to Emily.

Friends gave me a memory book for my birthday, and I spent the last months of Em's life gathering pictures and writing our story as a keepsake for myself. My most touching memories of the last month of Em's life were several times when I was sitting at her bedside when she was in a morphine-induced deep sleep. I began sobbing, wondering how I was going to live without her, how I was going to go on after she died. She awakened out of her comalike sleep, squeezed my hand, and told me that I was going to be okay. I believed that was a measure of her love for me, reaching out to reassure me while she was dying.

LOIS AND JOAN

Just as friends supported me as Em was dying, Lois experienced the support of friends during the time that Joan was dying, as well as afterward. Lois and Joan met in 1977 when Joan was twenty-nine and Lois was twenty-six. They were partnered for nineteen years, working together for thirteen of those nineteen years in their own home remodeling business. Lois wrote that they did not make much money but they enjoyed their work. They were also very active in the lesbian community and were organizers of the Midwest Women's Festival for many years. In addition, they were part of the Kansas City Women's Chorus for more than twelve years.

We were totally and completely out. We were featured in a TV news story on lesbian/gay long-term relationships in 1996. We were both out at our jobs, to our neighbors, etc. The last bastion of the closet was Joan's family . . . but we eventually did come out to them, thank goodness, several years before she got sick.

In May 1997, Joan went for a routine checkup that led to the discovery that she had ovarian cancer. She had a radical hysterectomy, followed by chemotherapy. After two months with no treatments, Joan was feeling stronger, so they went on vacation. "It was a wonderful time, incredibly sweet. We hiked up a ridge trail, went whale watching, and walked the beaches in the fog. But we returned to more bad news."

Tumors were found in Joan's lungs. After surgery to remove a lung, Lois wrote, "I began to understand that she was going to die." Then more tumors were found. Their friends formed a healing circle and Lois began sending out e-mail bulletins to friends and family.

Joan was never alone in the hospital, and she never touched the hospital food she hated. One blessed friend came every night to relieve me so I could go home to sleep and take care of the dogs. When I had to travel for business one time, Joan was scheduled for chemo, so one woman organized hospital room sitters for the whole week. We decorated her room every time she went in to make it more personal. We were completely out to all medical and insurance persons and never once had a negative experience. Everyone was very supportive and accepting.

A friend gave them the book *Close to the Bone* by Jean Shinoda Bolen, and Lois read it to Joan, a chapter a night.

Such a fortuitous journey! It gave us language and story, and connected us to mythic characters that gave us context for what we were going through. I realize now that we were talking mostly to each other, and each of us to one or two of our closest friends. It was incredibly intimate. We were, indeed, close to each other's bones.

They discovered other sources of support and comfort too.

During this time Joan began to work on unresolved wounds. Some she literally "fixed" with others involved. Other wounds we let go in healing rituals, just the two of us.

Hospice provided two key helps, in addition to the medical. The social worker and the play therapist were very helpful and supportive as my daughter and granddaughter came to terms with what was happening. And the music therapist was wonderful for Joan as she began to be more between the worlds. It seemed those hours of quiet piano gave Joan a chance to visit that state of consciousness.

There was also laughter to share.

Her tumors caused her to outgrow her jeans. I suggested she get some knit pants with elastic waists. Oh, no! She allowed as how she had always secretly admired a friend's wardrobe, sort of ethnic artsy long dresses. And so I took Joan, the quintessential butch in flannel and denim, to a boutique and we spent $250 on three lovely outfits. Then to a shoe store for a great pair of handmade German shoes to go with them. I wondered what the clerks thought, this tiny frail woman and her companion wiping away tears and both of them laughing.

Lois and Joan celebrated their anniversary for the last time, taking a picnic to the same apple orchard where they had celebrated their anniversary every year. Then they went to a benefit dance being held for them. Pictures taken that night suggest that friends were trying not to cry as they watched Joan and Lois dance around the floor one last time. Friends continued to surround them with love in the last days of Joan's life.

I had been imagining that I would take care of Joan alone until she died. Then I knew that wasn't right. The midwife image helped. Some years before we had been on a team assisting at a home birth for a lesbian mom and that's what we needed now, a team. We made up a list and called a meeting. Mostly these were good friends from chorus, my children, then twenty-eight and twenty-nine years old, and our granddaughter. Thirteen all together, including Joan.

For the remaining six days we were never alone. People slept whenever and wherever they could. One day we gathered around Joan and started singing, old songs for the chorus repertory, some folk music, some Broadway, some camp songs.

BEVERLY AND VIRGINIA

Whereas friends played a major role in my life and Lois's as our partner was dying, Beverly described a sense of intimacy in her caretaker role. Beverly was the oldest lesbian to contact me; she was sixty-three years old when her partner, Virginia, died at age sixty-nine. They had been together for almost thirty-seven years, the longest time of any couple in this book. It had only been six months since Virginia died when Beverly insisted she wanted to answer my questionnaire. Beverly identified Virginia as the love of her life, and her story of Virginia's illness and death is a testimony to the loving care Beverly gave to Virginia in her last days.

> I met the love of my life when I just happened to go with a friend of mine to visit a co-worker of hers. That co-worker was Virginia. Virginia was so feminine in dress and actions that I could not believe she was gay. But she was, and we became lovers not long after that. I was twenty-six; she was thirty-two and divorced, with a twelve-year-old son. As was typical at that time, we began living together right away, and although we agreed to make no commitment for the long term, we began mingling our incomes immediately.
>
> We were together thirty-six years and eight months when she passed away. We had many characteristics and preferences in common and where we differed, we usually complemented each other. This is not to say that everything went smoothly or perfectly. We had our ups and downs, but we had agreed to never go to bed angry, which turned out to work, since none of the things we argued over were important enough to keep us from being able to do that. We were very close. I accompanied her to every doctor's appointment and chemotherapy treatment during both the 1990-1991 and 1998-2002 periods. I was her only caretaker, which was a full-time job at first and then a twenty-four-hour-a-day, seven-days-a-week job for the last three months.

Prior to her recurrence, most of our future plans were just to continue our days doing the things we enjoyed, like reading, walking at the ocean or in the redwoods near our home, attending the lifelong learning groups we belonged to at the local community college, going to movies, plays, and concerts, and making a few trips. Even near the end, not that we knew it, we had plans to go see certain movies or eat at this place or that on her next "good day." We were out to our families, to close friends, and at work before we retired. We were not explicitly out to the older people we had met in the last few years. But we did not hide the fact that we had lived together all those years and did everything together.

She was diagnosed with stage two breast cancer in the mid-1990s and was treated with a mastectomy and six months of chemotherapy. In September 1998, her right femur broke, due to metastasic breast cancer. We knew that metastasis meant that she had a terminal illness, and we learned that she would be on chemotherapy for as long as she lived.

I did not really start preparing for her death until five months before her death. At that time, she went into shock after she had a surgery in which a liter of blood was drained from her right thigh. I realized that her health was so precarious; anything could take her at any time. I prepared over the next five months by trying to think about how it would be with her not being here in as many routine situations as I could.

She had been having trouble with infections for eight months and had been on antibiotics more than she was off during that time. Her thigh was infected, and I was giving her IV antibiotics every six hours around the clock. This procedure was supposed to last six weeks and we were just at the end of the third week when she passed away.

JANE AND LYNN

Although Beverly had a few months to prepare herself for Virginia's death, Lynn's death came more as a shock to Jane, even though Lynn had been sick for a while. Jane and Lynn were partnered for twenty-three years. They met initially when Jane was in a ballet class taught by Lynn. Six years later, Jane was unhappy at college, so she decided to contact Lynn, who was trying to start a small dance company in another state.

> While I was on a preliminary visit, she came out to me. I was sympathetic to her and we talked often on the phone for several months before I actually moved there. Within three or four days of arriving, we had coupled; I felt it was the most right thing I had ever done. It was 1976, and I was twenty-one; she was twenty-eight. She was the first woman I had ever been with.
>
> Our life was concentrated on dancing, developing a school and a small dance company. We taught in eight locations six days per week for that first year, driving together and hauling equipment together. I assisted in her classes, took class, rehearsed, became her muse. We were poor, but very happy. Within one year, we were formally married (to the extent that we could be at that time) in a Metropolitan Community Church. We chose to go to the other side of the state for safety reasons. To be "found out" in the dance-teaching profession in 1977 would have meant instant failure. The level of peace I felt at having professed our love and commitment was marked. I remember it to this day.
>
> For the next ten years, we worked together, developing a larger school and company, producing full-length ballets, learning and loving together. I was developing a talent for costuming, and assisted in many aspects of running the school and studio. Lynn's mother was also an integral part of this. Lynn was her only child, and her husband passed away two months before I arrived. There was also Lynn's business partner, Mary, who taught in the school. The four of us created a strong foursome team. This was (in my opinion) our happiest of years. We were strong, vibrant, enthusiastic, and very much in love. We were close physically, spending all of our waking and sleeping hours together, if not in the same room, certainly in the same building. It seemed to be against what most people told us to be true, that you can't work and live together and make it last. We did.
>
> Our life was full. We developed many friends, and during this time, I came out to my family. My sister and brother were always very supportive and nice to Lynn. My mother took it very poorly and could be quite rude. My dad, an Episcopalian minis-

ter who was divorced from my mother, kept his concerns to himself while he educated himself about homosexuality (as I later found out). He also became very fond of Lynn, recognizing the depth and quality of the relationship. Lynn never discussed our relationship with her mother, but I always felt welcome in her extended family.

Years later, Lynn contracted breast cancer and had a lumpectomy, followed by radiation and then chemotherapy, followed by five years of tamoxifen. Lynn then went back to school to complete a PhD. When she graduated, she worked for a consulting firm, and Jane returned to graduate school for a master's degree. Lynn's employer had questionable practices, however, and they kept changing health insurance companies and policies. Jane wrote:

> With Lynn, a good relationship with a doctor meant everything in trust and subsequently follow-up; so the checkups started to be farther and farther apart. I remember when we marked the "five years clear" point that she had not seen anyone for far more than six months. Somehow, there was a sense of doom in that.

Lynn developed a cough that did not go away. Tests indicated that she again had cancer, breast cancer that had now settled in the lungs. She was admitted to the hospital to determine how extensively the cancer had spread. Jane wrote that the hospital stay was a blur:

> I had no concept of the time. I just felt like I had spent hours trying to calm her and create a soft, warm environment so that she would not think about her ailments. She spoke several times about things that made little sense to me. I realized she was having conversations in her head from times past or about things left unsaid. Finally, after some amount of trouble and her breathing becoming more labored, she uttered one word. At the time I believed she said "Die," but I think now it was "Bye."
>
> I was trying to get her attention, holding her shoulders and looking into her eyes when I saw the whites turn yellow and knew she had passed. I cried for at least half an hour alone by her side. I think I might have fallen asleep on her chest for at least a time. I wanted so much to feel her breathing again.

Jane wrote to me three years after Lynn's death and shared her reflections on what had happened during that time:

> There was no time to prepare. We did not talk about the possibility of death because I do not think either of us really could believe that might be a possibility. I always wondered if she knew deep inside about her own health status. For about a year or so I thought the death took her by surprise, but I have changed my mind on that and think she likely knew she was slipping from this life. She made a valiant effort to stay, but in the end she knew that the quality of life would not be as she would want and decided to let go.

Jane described the time around Lynn's death as a blur, while Nora wrote about how frenzied the time was for her as she was faced with Anne's imminent death:

> I think I was driven by the fact that I had not been able to do enough for my son. I became distraught, trying to go back and forth between my house and hers, run a business, and care for Anne. I visited her daily. One day I got a call from hospice saying that she had died at 5:00 a.m. I was horrified. I rushed to the hospice but found that there had been a mix-up and that was not true. But when I entered her room, I realized that Anne really was already dead. I think she wanted to be alone at that moment.

Nora, like many of us, juggled caretaking with a job and other responsibilities. Still, Anne's fight to survive ended, and Nora's hopes for a future together were dashed. Marilyn also had a hectic caretaking schedule. In addition to caring for Cheryl as she was dying, she had the care of their three adult children with disabilities.

> It was a difficult, crazy schedule: get the boys up, get myself dressed, get Cheryl dressed and downstairs before leaving for work at 7:00 a.m. When I got home, I showered, spent some time with Cheryl, made dinner, went food shopping as needed, put the kids to bed, put Cheryl to bed, and collapsed. I was the sole caregiver. Cheryl would not let me bring in any help.
> The absolute hardest part of her dying was that our relationship had become platonic for some years before she became ill.

As I cared for her and shared her fear, I so wanted to love her intimately, to hold her and kiss her over and over. But she only had enough energy to try to beat death. I wanted to talk about our life together and all we had meant to each other and had accomplished together, but that would have meant her admitting she was dying and she just could not accept that.

Once in awhile out of desperation I would say, "I might as well go back to work and hire a caregiver. You don't need someone to love you, just someone to be your arms and legs." But then she would cry and say, "I do love you," so I guess I will just have to remember that.

The pain of watching Cheryl die and being exhausted with her caretaking role were major parts of Marilyn's experience. But this already difficult time was complicated more by Cheryl's stubborn refusal to allow anyone else to help her or to even talk about dying.

IRENE AND MJ

In MJ's case, Irene related that, even though MJ had been sick for a while, neither one of them prepared for her death because they kept focusing on MJ's fight to live. After all, she had already successfully fought one round of cancer. Irene wrote the following about their relationship:

We met playing softball together on the same team. I played third base and MJ played shortstop. How could I not notice her? She was tall and fit, with beautiful green eyes and long dark hair. She was very kind and friendly; everyone liked MJ. Still, it took several months for us to grow close and come out to each other. We were twenty-eight and thirty-one, and it was MJ's first committed lesbian relationship. We were together all the time for the first nine months, then we moved in together.

It was a wonderful relationship from the start. We were very compatible; the energy and chemistry was there for both of us. I knew this was special. We were together for twenty years and traveled extensively together, had many friends, and were out or at least open to most all of our family and straight friends. We planned to grow old together.

During our late forties we looked forward to eventual career changes from our corporate jobs and a long happy retirement. We were blessed and knew it. Others told us we were a model for them in the way we lived our lives together. Later they told me I was a model for how to love someone so deeply and let go with dignity. The first part was so easy and the last was painful beyond imagining, like a price to pay for having been given so much.

MJ experienced a diagnosis of a benign breast growth and a subsequent surgery around age thirty-seven. We hoped it was not a forewarning of a more serious illness to come, and she took care to have annual mammograms. In the summer of 1992 her father passed away at age seventy-two after a prolonged struggle with heart disease. Only six months later her mother was diagnosed with lung cancer and died in the fall of 1993. MJ was deeply saddened and depressed following the trauma of such loss. She was especially close to her mother, who died at the young age of sixty-seven. MJ's health and well-being had been compromised through the stress of the ordeal.

In the spring of 1994 she herself was diagnosed with breast cancer at the age of forty-five. She rallied from her depression to bravely face the battle of her life. Through three surgeries, chemotherapy, and radiation she never wavered in her courage, resolve, and good spirits. She was determined to live. Following her recovery from treatments, she lived her life fully, but the cancer was too aggressive to be contained. Four years later she was diagnosed with breast cancer metastasized to her liver. The proliferation of the disease in this vital organ was extensive.

MJ rallied once again to face a formidable foe. She endured high-level chemotherapy treatments. She never gave up hope for her ability to survive with the disease and have more time. She had plans for the new millennium. In a few months she was in dire straits from the traumatic effects of both the cancer and the treatments. We never talked about dying, and she cried when she was told there were no more treatments that could help her. Her heart was broken. In February 1999, her liver failed following a desperate attempt to endure oral chemotherapy. In two weeks she was gone. We buried her in her hometown. She was only fifty years old. I was forty-eight but felt like ninety.

Forty-eight but feeling like ninety. Another way of expressing the exhaustion we felt from caretaking and loss. That theme of exhaustion was part of the story for all of us who found ourselves in a caregiver role—exhaustion from the hectic physical schedules we kept, and exhaustion from the emotional drain of watching our partner slowly die.

LINDA AND TONYA

In Linda's case, Tonya's death resulted not from a terminal illness but from complications from gastric bypass surgery. Tonya was only thirty-eight years old, and the last thing on their minds when she had surgery was any consideration that she might die. Linda and Tonya had been friends for several years, visiting occasionally, mainly calling and e-mailing since they lived in different states. They were both partnered with other women during this time, and the four of them enjoyed each other's company. Of Tonya, Linda wrote,

> Tonya was the first lesbian I had ever met that I could have an intelligent conversation with on almost any subject, including computers, which was my specialty. Tonya talked about the classes she was taking to obtain her EdD.

First Tonya's partner left her, and Linda became Tonya's shoulder to cry on. Then Linda's partner left her, and Tonya sympathized and listened. When they finally became lovers, it was a commuter relationship until Tonya relocated and moved in with Linda. Linda was a little nervous about that.

> Having Tonya move in was a big step for me as I had not felt that anyone I had lived with and been involved with in the past had worked out. Adjusting to having another person in a one-bedroom apartment was interesting since Tonya and I were polar opposites. She lived with piles everywhere and I was the neat freak.

In addition to a teaching position, Tonya began a business buying and selling on the Internet.

At first I kept saying, "This is not going to work." That was be-cause I had a previous girlfriend who had tried to have a busi-ness on the side and it did not work, but Tonya soon proved me wrong. We were starting to see our dreams come true. We wanted to buy a home and did. As Tonya became more confi-dent in her life, she came out with a bang, while I was not ex-actly advertising my preferences. I worked in a corporate world where my sexual orientation was not exactly accepted.

Tonya had battled all her life with her weight. Linda explained why Tonya decided to undergo gastric bypass surgery and how what should have been a relatively simple procedure turned into one com-plication after another.

She once told me that she believed her weight issues started back when she was three years old. After many diets, fad diets, and twelve-step programs, she had decided that gastric bypass was her only option left.

The day after Tonya had gastric bypass surgery, she was in the intensive care unit, needing dialysis and oxygen support. It seems as if her kidneys had started shutting down, plus her asthma had kicked up. After four or five days in the intensive care unit, she was transferred back to a regular floor and room. The one-time dialysis treatment seemed to work, but she still needed oxygen—so they were going to keep her in the hospital a while longer.

A few days later, Tonya began experiencing pains in her stomach. The nurses told her it was just gas and to get up and walk. She did, but by the next morning she still wasn't feeling any better. She called me and asked me to get to the hospital ASAP. The surgeons performed several tests and decided they needed to take her back to surgery since she had peritonitis. It seems as if one of the internal staples had come apart, and she was leaking bowel contents into her insides.

Tonya called her brother and asked him to come, since there was a real possibility that she could die from this. He arrived minutes before Tonya was wheeled back to the intensive care unit. He was a minister, and his presence was of great comfort to Tonya. He spent the nights at the hospital, so I could go home and get some rest.

Tonya survived this incident, but, for the next few months, every time it looked like Tonya was getting better, another setback would occur. There were more surgeries, more back and forth between home and hospital. Once again, Tonya seemed to get better, and then her kidneys began to fail and she had a high fever. Linda called her family, friends, and Tonya's friends to let them know what was happening.

> When I arrived to talk to her, I asked if she had any fight left in her. Her response was "No." She asked my permission to go, which, knowing her wishes, I gave. It was the hardest thing I have ever done.

For many of us, there came a time when we had to let go and allow our partner to die. And it truly was the hardest thing we had ever done.

EXAMPLES OF SUPPORT

Some of the lesbian widows who contacted me had the support of family, friends, and the medical establishment while their partner was sick and dying. Others did not. Vera's story is an example of someone who received that kind of support.

> Nancy changed a lot of the ways that she ate and she exercised, something she had not done before. We had a healing circle going every day at seven o'clock; we had a lot of women sending her healing energy.
>
> I just cannot even imagine what it would have been like for people not to have known that I was her partner, and no one ever, ever gave us any trouble or anything. We had medical powers of attorney for each other, which Nancy always presented to the doctor or the hospital, whatever it was. I was just matter-of-factly treated as her spouse by everybody around. Nancy was not very close to her family, and so they were never around during any of the medical procedures, and that was fine with me.

Heather likewise talked about being out and accepted. She was a graduate student when Ruth was dying and related a funny incident that occurred:

We were both out as lesbians. I cannot imagine having struggled through this without those in my life knowing what was going on. Sometimes they only found out when I explained the reason I failed to meet a responsibility. I had to chuckle over one conversation.

I was a graduate student doing some research for a psychologist and had to call her to cancel a meeting. I told her I was in the emergency room because of a medical crisis with my lover. She was very gracious, and the next time she saw me asked how my mother was doing. I was very confused (my mother having died a few years before that) until I realized what she misheard. A lesson about Freud from a psychologist who heard what was more comfortable.

EXAMPLES OF ISOLATION

On the other hand, some lesbian widows suffered because they were lesbian. Traci, for example, was a teacher who kept her relationship with Dana private. She wrote about what she did as Dana was dying:

> Having to keep this to myself was impossible. So through my daily tears I had to say something. I announced that my sister was dying. Now I could keep my job as an educator and get support from my colleagues. It was acceptable to have a dying sister, not a dying partner.

Emily and I told the surgeon and other hospital personnel that we were sisters. That is what Cheryl and Marilyn also did when Cheryl was diagnosed with ALS. Later, when Cheryl needed around-the-clock care, Marilyn decided to leave her job and stay home to take care of her. She experienced discrimination when she was denied family leave because their relationship was not legally recognized as a marriage. "I took a personal leave from work, but I was denied family leave. That meant no salary and no COBRA benefits."

In an already upsetting situation, Marilyn had to struggle with employment and financial concerns in a way that a married widow would not. Like Marilyn, Ellen was not out at work, but she came out after Kate's tragic death.

I was a nurse, and the hospital I was working at was very conservative. I did not feel free to be out at work. And that is something no straight couple would have to deal with. I came out in
the tragedy of her death. I felt vulnerable and exposed at every
level, but I did not care at that point. And I actually did not lose
my job.

To my face, people were kind; I did not know if there was talk
behind my back. It was the emotional thing of exposure at the
worst time in my life. I told the story over and over, but in telling
the story of her death over and over at work and coming out at
the same time, it felt traumatic. They would say, "I am sorry
about what happened to your friend."

Even in their expression of sympathy, however, Ellen's colleagues
did not recognize Kate as her spouse, only as a friend. That had the effect of minimizing the importance of the relationship to Ellen. The
death of a friend, even a close one, is not equivalent to the death of a
spouse.

As the end got closer for Emily, I did not know how well I would be
functioning when Emily died, or whether I would be able to work. So
I decided to break my silence at work. I came out to my department
chair and one other faculty person. They were extremely supportive
and encouraged me to come out to the rest of the faculty because they
believed everyone else would also be supportive. But I did not have
the emotional energy at that time to take that risk. At least now my department chair knew what was going on and was prepared to step in
and provide whatever relief I might need at work.

At the most painful time in our lives, some of us were treated as if
we did not exist, faced having our relationship ignored or minimized,
or felt forced to come out to obtain help. One caretaker was denied
family leave. Married women do not face these issues. Their relationships and their grief are publicly recognized and honored.

It is interesting to note that the majority of the widows in this book
were out and experienced no discrimination. It was primarily those of
us who were not out who encountered problems. However, the reason
that so many lesbians were out and received support, I believe, reflects the historical time in which these events happened. Such open-
ness would not have been possible twenty, thirty, forty years ago.

Chapter 6

Parting Moments

In the last weeks of Emily's life, I found myself having to comfort people who visited and saw how terrible she looked. When the doctor predicted she had only one week left, her mother and sister flew in from out of state, but Emily continued to be stubborn and lived another three weeks. She asked me to send roses and thank-you notes to all the friends who had supported her through this time. A nice final gesture, I thought. Before Em slipped into a coma during the last few days of her life, I wrote in my journal:

Yesterday I cuddled up next to Em in her bed for a while. It was nice. We talked and cried together. We assured each other of our love. It may be the last chance we have to do that.

We have said what we wanted to say to each other; I am ready to let her go. But as I sit here with her, a part of me wants to rage—and does at times—Why does such a good person have to die so young? Why does this brilliant, well-loved woman have to suffer and die? It is so unfair. And yet one of the surprising things I have learned from all this is that dying is sacred, not a tragedy.

I feel privileged to be accompanying Em in her dying process, even though it is hard and it does not make sense that she is dying so young. It has been a sacred experience. Yet I can hardly bear it when I think of being left alone when Em dies. I know that, in the long run, I will be okay, but the hole in my heart will be enormous.

THE PRESENCE OF DEATH

During that last week, when I was sitting in the room watching her sleep, I had the sense that Death was hovering over her in the room. I do not know how else to explain it. It was not frightening, just a very definite Presence. I knew the end was near. And I knew that I was experiencing something sacred. Donna also mentioned a spiritual aspect to their experience:

Traditional Western medicine and alternative therapies had been tried. Our hopes and dreams and prayers also did not cure the cancer. We talked, saw friends and relatives, made a final journey to California. We chose in-home hospice care, and asked for a nurse with a wry sense of humor. We got one! We invited Randi's daughter and daughter's partner to be with us. The four of us (three Sagittarians and a Scorpio) were a powerful force. Death was a worthy opponent turned friend.

In addition, Donna related an unexpected source of comfort to her as Randi was dying:

Music had always been a salvation for me; one of my jobs was singing in a choir. [She had several part-time jobs.] I told the choir director that Randi was dying and I could not reliably predict whether I would be able to show up on a future date, or, if there, be able to sing. I offered to find a permanent substitute for myself until such time as my life became more stable. He was marvelously understanding and flexible, and told me that I could just see how I felt every day, and come sing or not, no advance notice required, no need to find a substitute. This was one of the most helpful things anyone did for me. As it happened, I think I only missed one day. And the music was a balm and a healing influence for me.

I experienced Death as a sacred presence while Donna described it as a worthy opponent turned friend. These are not the typical American attitudes toward death.

A SPIRITUAL EXPERIENCE

Maureen described the spiritual experience she had at the time of Robin's death. First she shared what occurred during Robin's last days and then what happened the night that Robin passed away.

As the days went by, Robin lost more and more control of everything. One day she could go to the bathroom herself, the next day she needed everyone to lift her from the bed and set her on a bedside commode, and the next day she was using a bedpan.

The progression was so fast once they stopped treating the cancer.

I took a leave of absence from work and spent twenty-four hours a day taking care of her. Her children and I called everyone and had a big going-away party for Robin. People from all stages of her life came together to celebrate her life before she was not able to celebrate with them. This was the first time she ever really let her friends from grade school, from work, etc., really know *who* Robin was . . . a lesbian.

During this time we also planned her funeral and took care of a lot of details we needed to do. She told her sons where she wanted to be buried. She picked her own tombstone. She called a friend to ask her to sing at the funeral. She picked the songs to be sung. She helped us to prepare for life without her. She told everyone good-bye and what they meant to her.

She had not spoken or responded for a couple days. I went to let the dog out in the backyard, and the sky was so beautiful. The stars were bright and the moon was lighting up the whole sky. I turned around and said to her, "Robin, you should see how great the sky looks out here. It is so beautiful. You would love it." When I turned around, her daughter told me that Robin had stopped breathing. I feel like she really went to look and see the sky we had spent so many nights sitting under and dancing in the backyard. Somehow it made me feel better.

Robin faced death bravely, saying good-bye to her loved ones and leaving specific directions regarding her funeral. Despite the pain and shock Maureen felt when she first realized that Robin was going to die, Maureen experienced a moment of peace as Robin took her last breath. Anna Marie explained how Caroline fought to stay lucid in order to say good-bye to family and friends. In doing so, Caroline was able to depart with peace in her heart.

She would not take any medication. She would not take morphine for the pain. She said she did not want it. Everybody had their time to talk with her. Only then did she ask the nurse for the pain shot and she went to sleep. I thought she was just resting peacefully. The death rattle. I will never forget it. I called for the nurse to come in right away, but that was it. She was gone.

Caroline somehow knew what she needed to do before she could leave; she needed to say a final farewell to those she loved.

SAYING GOOD-BYE

For Joan, there were many layers of preparation and a great deal of support as she breathed her last. Lois described how friends and hospice workers participated in Joan's passing.

> By Saturday she was barely conscious and her breathing was steadily more difficult. I do not know how many hours we sang to her, a core group of probably ten or so. A friend who came in described the scene around Joan as having an incredible golden aura. The hypnotist we had worked with came and led all of us through a wonderful guided imagery that was about all of us going so far with Joan, and then releasing her to go on ahead. We took turns going out of the room to cry or rest.
>
> At some point I called hospice and described her symptoms and our caregiving. The nurse confirmed that we were doing fine and asked if I thought we needed her. I said, "No." We agreed to continue to give her the liquid morphine, enough to ensure that she was not struggling or in pain.
>
> Joan had gotten pretty messy, and we decided to clean her up. She was fastidious in her personal habits and we thought it would be what she wanted. To avoid disturbing her, we actually cut the sweat suit she was wearing to pieces. We sponged her off, and changed the bedding. We did not try to redress her, just snuggled her into a blanket.

Lois had just decided to lie down and rest when someone came to get her because Joan was breathing her last breaths. Lois described Joan's final moments and then related what they did in the hours immediately after Joan passed away:

> She went very gently, a seemingly perceptible shrinking as her spirit left her body. We each spent time sitting alone with Joan's body and then got ready to wash her. Great care was taken to develop a scented oil that she liked. We put her body on a massage table and gathered round.

I do not know if I can really describe the ritual of saying good-bye to Joan's body. I washed her, speaking to every part as I did so. I remember telling the cancer that it had thoroughly wasted its efforts to take over her body since it died when she died. Friends washed her hair. We all oiled her, singing. And we dressed her in her favorite soft cotton long underwear and a pair of woolly socks. She did not want to have cold feet! I leaned over her to kiss her one more time, and then an old song came to me: "Sisters, you keep me fighting, you keep me strong."

Singing had played a major role in Lois and Joan's relationship, and song rose up within Lois at the time of their final parting. Like Joan, Nancy was surrounded by a community of friends as she breathed her last. Vera explained,

> It had been clear all day that she was dying. A bunch of our friends were at the hospital, and I just got this brainstorm and said to the doctor, "Could we stand around the bed?" He said sure, so he said good-bye to her and he left.
>
> I think there were about a dozen of us, and we surrounded the bed. It was a Catholic hospital, but no one ever gave me any trouble for being her partner. No one ever gave me any trouble when I agreed that it was time to turn off the machines. In fact, they gave her morphine, because I was really afraid it would be a hard death. And so the most fabulous nurse in intensive care eased the passage. So when Nancy died, she was completely surrounded by twelve loving women friends.

MEMORIES AND LAUGHTER

Although Nancy and Joan were surrounded by friends at the time of their death, Randi was encircled by her family. Laughter had been an important part of Donna and Randi's relationship, and it also played a role as Randi prepared to leave. At the beginning of their relationship, they had begun to feel like they were wearing a path in the road between their homes, so they bought one together. So in addition to laughter, Donna found that good memories of their time together helped ease her pain.

Moving into our own house gave us more time together. I am glad now that we were so intensely involved and could spend almost all of our time together. That gave me a large bank of happy memories to draw upon.

Less than four years after they met, they learned that Randi had cancer, which had spread to her lungs and was no longer treatable. Donna shared the positive way they faced Randi's death:

Randi planned and participated in her dying process. It was a fine example to us of a positive model for dying. Anger, grieving, and acceptance were mixed together. If Randi could not continue to live in a way that was joyous to her, we all agreed that death perhaps was a reasonable alternative, or perhaps the only one. There are possibilities worse than death—incapacity, helplessness, pain.

Death was no exception to our policy of enjoying everything and laughing as much as possible. When we heard that she would die, the first thing she said was, "Oh good! No cataract surgery."

We invited her daughter Jean and Jean's partner David to be with us at the end. David and Jean brought a blank notebook, some scissors, glue, markers, pens. They invited everyone who came to visit to write or draw something in the book. Randi got to read it and participate in the making of the book. Later, it became a repository of good memories, a comfort, and a companion to cry with.

Our four cats participated in her death as much as they chose to. They came in and out of the room, slept on the bed, were cuddled. When Randi died, it was in the embrace of three people and one cat.

A SENSE OF INTIMACY

In Donna's story, I can sense the love and tenderness that was present in Randi's parting moment. Likewise, Samantha related the intimacy she and Marie felt just before Marie passed away. On Christmas Eve, Samantha fixed a nice dinner, even though Marie was only able to eat a couple of bites.

She told me then that she felt loved and safe in the home that I had created for us. After that she lost touch. She died that evening. Her best friend remained with me to offer support and to witness this passing. When she died, I cried as hard as I ever have because I knew that it would not hurt her and that I could finally kiss her without fear of causing her pain. It was a relief and an utter devastation. I was numb after that and completely exhausted.

A relief and an utter devastation. Both at the same time. A good description of the final farewell. Although Randi was surrounded by family, and Joan and Nancy were surrounded by friends, Beverly was alone with Virginia when she died.

That morning I could not wake her when I gave her the 6:00 a.m. antibiotic. I tried every half hour to wake her up. I thought I could not do so because of the high amount of pain medication she was on, so I took the pain patch off. At 1:00 p.m. her breathing was so shallow, I called her doctor and was on the phone to him when she appeared to quit breathing altogether.

What helped me most immediately was the nurse who came. Of course I was crying. She hugged me and then helped me call the funeral home. As soon as Betty, Virginia's sister, got here, she called one of their relatives, who called other family members, including Virginia's son. And I had seven of them with me all afternoon. And then on Monday, her son Steve went with me to the funeral home. At Virginia's request, we had just a small memorial service at home the following Saturday. And I arranged to have some food brought in so we could eat here afterward.

Beverly's story makes it clear what a difference it makes when family members, medical personnel, and funeral homes accept a lesbian relationship and offer their support to the widowed partner. Beverly was fortunate to receive the kind of help that most married widows take for granted, even though she was a lesbian. Like Beverly, Marilyn was alone with her partner when Cheryl died.

She slept almost all day, breathing shallowly. We needed to turn her over on her side to change the bed and something happened at that moment. I'm guessing it was her heart that absolutely terrified her. Her pulse raced and a look of panic came over her face. A tear fell from her eyes and she grabbed onto me without saying a word. We settled her, and I held her for a few moments and she fell asleep. I knew she would die that night. I can't tell you how I knew, but I knew the exact moment that she slipped from sleep into a coma and from coma to brain dead. I knew that her last breath was her last, and I also felt the presence of God.

Many of the widows in this book were present at the moment of their partner's passing, but that was not true for everyone. Pam was not in the room when Sandy died but spent time with Sandy's body after Sandy stopped breathing.

Sandy had always been afraid that, if something were to happen to her, she would have no one to care for her since both her parents were dead and she was an only child. I had promised her I would always be there for her and I kept my promise. I did it all for love.

She died with one friend in the room, the pastor of the local Metropolitan Community Church (MCC). I wondered if she had to wait until she could slip away with someone who wasn't a family member. We all had some time with her after she passed. The local Jewish funeral home was called, and they came and got her body. The staff at the funeral home was very respectful of me. I was treated as Sandy's spouse and next of kin.

Pam speculated that maybe Sandy needed to wait until no family members were present before she could leave. I had wondered the same thing about Emily. She passed away in the middle of the night when I was asleep in another room and only the nighttime nurse's aide was with her. Similar to Pam, I too spent time alone with Emily's body before her family joined me and before we called the funeral home.

As with many of the stories already shared in this chapter, Pat discovered that, despite her fears, she had no trouble with health care professionals or funeral home directors not honoring her relationship to Betty.

In the late evening, after Betty had gone into the coma, a friend of ours helped me to find a funeral home that would be respectful of our relationship. Although her brother and I were a bit apprehensive when we went to the funeral home the next day, there was no problem of any note. I went armed with all the documents I had, the power of attorney and her will, to bolster my statements of Betty's intent that I should make all pertinent decisions. The funeral director conferred with his advisor and determined that the documentation was adequate to preclude any assertion of parental rights and we proceeded as I wished.

THE RELATIONSHIP NOT RECOGNIZED

Although she had anticipated problems, Pat's relationship to Betty was respected. In contrast, Dale shared how she was discriminated against when Carol died. This discrimination only increased her level of pain.

> It was difficult watching her fade away by inches. The arrangements after her death were another pain. The first funeral home I went to refused to pick up her body unless [the request] was signed by a blood relative. I did not count as one even though I was the executor of her will, had control of what little money there was, and also had all forms of power of attorney. I did finally find [a funeral home] that would do as I asked.

Anita also experienced discrimination, not by a funeral home but by the hospital and Holly's brother, who completely ignored who Anita was. When she arrived at the hospital, after her two-hour commute, she was stunned to learn that Holly had already passed away. "The hospital was just keeping her alive until her brother could come from Florida to take care of business. I was completely left out. I had nothing."

THE PAINFUL REALITY

In sharing our experiences of the time of death of our partner, it feels to me like these words on paper do not begin to convey the depth of the pain that I was feeling or what other lesbian widows felt when their partner died, whether anticipated or not. Just as Ellen wrote how her words describing Kate sounded so lifeless compared to the lively person that Kate really was (Chapter 2), so too words cannot convey the intensity of the ache in losing one's partner.

The pain I experienced over Em's death seemed both emotional and physical to me. It felt like someone had ripped out part of my heart, leaving an open, gaping wound. Nora described her pain this way: "The pain was more excruciating than any physical pain I have ever experienced." Ellen elaborated:

> Previously I had grandparents and aunts and a cousin die, and I felt like I had been through this before. But I had not. It is the level of closeness. It was so much more intense than any other experience.

Rose had the unfortunate experience of being widowed twice, first as a married woman and then as a lesbian. She wrote, "My sense of anguish and loss this time was completely overwhelming, far, far greater than anything I had felt when my husband died." This is not to say that married widows do not also experience intense pain. Grief authors talk about how women, in general, grieve differently from men. Doka (2002) called women intuitive grievers while men are instrumental grievers; in essence, women "feel" and men "do." Intuitive grievers "experience and express grief as deep feeling" (p. 14). Walter (2003) wrote, "The loss of a partner is always highly traumatic. The beliefs, assumptions, and expectations regarding ourselves and the world around us are shattered. Bereaved partners are forced to make sense of experiences that seem senseless" (p. xvi).

The death of our partner at such a young age really did seem senseless to us. And in the months after that loss, we struggled to find new meaning for our lives. Fortunately, the majority of lesbians included in this book were out and had no problems with medical or funeral personnel at the time their lover passed away. Only one lesbian, Dale, mentioned being discriminated against by a funeral home, and Anita faced discrimination by the hospital and Holly's family.

Chapter 7

Funerals and Memorial Services

For the twenty-five women, including myself, whose stories are in this book, there were twenty-five unique rituals to commemorate the death of our loved one. For some, the funerals or memorial services were very meaningful experiences. For others, they were nightmares. In my case, friends and family honored Emily's passing three different times.

A visitation was held the night before the funeral. Em's family put together collages of pictures and awards and memorabilia of her life, and hundreds of people paid their respects. I was touched that the two colleagues to whom I had come out at work attended the visitation. It also meant a lot to me that my brother and sister-in-law came. Even though I was not out to them, my brother had helped nurse a friend of his who had died of cancer, so he knew that this had been a difficult time for me. Our lesbian friends were there in force and assured me of their support. I came home exhausted but deeply touched.

The church was packed for the funeral the next day. Em had been well loved by everyone who knew her; her colleagues, students, and friends filled the pews. Her family fully included me in all these events and I sat with them during the service. Most of the people who attended the funeral probably did not know who I was or why I was sitting with the family since Emily was not out at work. But the people who were closest to us knew. It was a very emotional service for me, and I wept through most of it. My minister told me afterward that she could not look at me when she was speaking or she would not have been able to get through her eulogy. Emily had arranged for the minister at my Unitarian-Universalist church to play a role at the funeral at her Methodist church since she had attended many activities at my church with me. Both her minister and mine tactfully mentioned me in their sermons, for which I was grateful.

Almost every day during the week after her death I had friends take me to lunch or dinner or for walks, talk to me, encourage me, check in on me. But I still felt like something was missing. Although the visitation and funeral service had been wonderful celebrations of Emily's life, they were not open celebrations of us as a lesbian couple. I decided that I needed to have a private memorial service with just our lesbian friends. Three weeks after her death, nineteen women met with me to honor Emily. My journal entry afterward read:

> We sat in a circle and shared our memories of Em. I shared the story of our relationship. Many did not know it since Em had been so unwilling to come out to anyone, even lesbian friends. So it ended up being a coming-out party for me as well as a memorial for Em. As each one reminisced about Em, we laughed together and we cried together. Several talked about sensing Em's presence since her death.
>
> At the end, we held hands and spoke a blessing to everyone in the circle: Peace, Compassion, Community, etc. I sensed Em's presence and the gift of community.

FEELING INVISIBLE

Although my experiences at the visitation, funeral, and memorial service were all affirmative, not everyone had such positive experiences. Maureen, for example, described how Robin's family treated her.

> Robin's brother gave her eulogy and listed me as her "dear friend" or something like that. I was just happy to be acknowledged by them at all. She had never told her kids, family, friends, co-workers, or anyone else about us except a few close friends. Her sons never said anything to me to let on that they even knew or suspected. I am not really sure who they thought I was if not their mom's lover.

Not having the relationship acknowledged is a very painful experience at a time when we are already in pain. Similar to Maureen, Traci was not accepted as Dana's partner. Before her death, Dana picked out her headstone and decided on the particulars for her funeral, so Traci thought everything was set. Instead, she found that Dana's family took over and made her feel invisible.

The day of the funeral came. Dana's ex-husband and three children arrived at my home. The first thing out of her ex-husband's mouth was, "I have an attorney!" I stood there with my mouth open.

Upon my arrival at the funeral home, photos of Dana, her ex-husband, and her children were displayed. There were no photos of Dana and me together. Her mother and sister saw to that. I was not mentioned at the service, and the song Dana had chosen was not played. Rather a religious song and speech were given. Dana was not a religious woman and did not want a religious ceremony. Her family had won.

Traci perceived the cruel behavior of Dana's ex-husband and other family members as the triumph of Dana's heterosexual past being recognized, but her lesbian relationship with Traci being denied. This seems a clear reflection of Dana's family's homophobia and lack of acceptance of Dana's partnership. Like Traci, Heather thought everything was taken care of before the funeral, but she too found out otherwise. Ruth and Heather had been partnered for twelve years before Ruth died of complications from diabetes. Ruth wanted to be cremated, and Heather arranged it.

Ruth had not said what should be done with the ashes, and I had not thought to ask. It turned into a big family argument. Some wanted to bury the ashes in the family plot where Ruth's father was buried and her mother eventually would be. Others were opposed, saying that her father would not have wanted her buried with them since he disapproved of her lesbianism. But she *did* end up in the family plot, and I have not been there since.

There is a sense of betrayal in both Heather's and Traci's experiences. The family of origin's wishes prevailed over the wishes of their lesbian daughter and their daughter's partner. In a similar vein, Linda was hurt by how Tonya's family treated her.

Of the people who came to the memorial service, I did not know 99 percent of them. Tonya's relatives felt that acknowledging who I was in their church would be disconcerting, so I was relegated to "nobody" status.

Nobody status. Another way of saying that the relationship between Linda and Tonya was not acknowledged because Tonya's family was unable to accept their lesbian relationship. In a similar way, Holly's family ignored Anita. Yet Anita and her friends found a way to memorialize Holly.

> We waited for them [Holly's family] to come back [from the church and cemetery], then we went there and did our own thing. I had about eight friends come with me. We went to eat after the Mass and then we went to the cemetery plot. The grave was still open and the casket was down in it. We threw things down there for Holly. She was a smoker, so I gave her a cigarette lighter. One of my friends gave her a quarter to put in the slots. That was funny. So we were not part of Holly's funeral but I felt okay with that.

HURT BY LESBIANS

Although some lesbians felt slighted or hurt by family members, Samantha and Ellen were hurt by their fellow lesbians.

> I was so numb after Marie's death and so completely exhausted that Marie's friends planned the memorial service and I went through the legal motions required. Marie was to be cremated and half her remains returned to Peru. With all that arranged, I went to the memorial service thinking that I could not bring myself to stand up in front of anyone to say anything. I was spent but I knew in my heart of hearts that I had done everything that I could to ensure that Marie knew she was loved and protected and taken care of to the best of my ability. Marie had acknowledged that Christmas Eve. In this respect I was at ease.
>
> The memorial service was in a beautiful Unitarian church and people got up and said what they needed to. I sat and listened. At the end of the service I realized that not one person, gay or straight, had so much as mentioned my name as ever being a part of Marie's life or having anything to do with it. One of her professors and friends mentioned "the blossoming love" between Marie and her previous marriage partner that she had stayed with for barely two years, but no mention at all was made of me. I never have felt so completely nullified in my life. I had

never ever felt so let down by both my own people and everyone that had known either of us.

I had no idea how to respond or react. I was crushed into another space of nonexistence. After it was all over, I closed the door to my house and retreated into myself. I felt so let down by everyone that I wanted nothing to do with anyone. I went back to work and did what I had to do to survive but nothing more.

Samantha felt invisible at the funeral service when there was no recognition of her relationship with Marie, not even from friends. And not just invisible, but also betrayed by friends from whom she had expected to receive support. Ellen was also hurt by fellow lesbians when Kate's friends talked about "the good old days" with Kate, ignoring Ellen as the spouse.

At the funeral, I was another person for the week. I was child-like, simple, no sense of social connection as I floated through the week. Like a state of grace. Almost as if I had died myself. I had a sense of sweet acceptance of everyone who came up to me yet I was unable to say anything to anyone. Lots of Kate's friends and former lovers came to the funeral. Some were part of Kate's lesbian AA subgroup.

We did a memorial service later on the day of the funeral. Women got up and shared about their past with Kate, perhaps having a fling with her, talking about drinking together, and then recovery together. The memorial was almost like an AA meeting, even though Kate had been in recovery fifteen years. This would not have happened at a heterosexual gathering. People would have felt it was inappropriate to talk about having had flings or getting drunk with her in the past when they were younger. The sense in the group was that her death had an impact on their community. One friend told me she felt they should have had more respect for me as her partner. But they acted like Kate was theirs.

OPEN SUPPORT

In contrast to Ellen's and Samantha's negative experiences with fellow lesbians, Lois was fully supported and assisted by friends in memorializing Joan. Prior to Joan's death, friends helped make and decorate a casket for her. When she died, friends helped wash and prepare the body. The next morning, friends ritually took Joan's body to the funeral home, and the following Sunday, a memorial service was held in her honor.

A cabinet shop made us a simple plywood box, sized to fit her, and Constance brought it to our basement workshop. Our son primed it; our friend Karen designed and sketched the exterior decoration, using the Neon Girl character. We all painted it in tempera, bright purple and green mostly, with dogs cavorting around the sides.

Our friend Deb talked about wanting to send a message with Joan, to write it in her own hand, and that gave me an idea for the inside of the box. I asked people to draw around their hands and write a message to Joan inside. The phone tree was activated, and I sent an e-mail to our list. That was on Tuesday. By Saturday we had 250 hands. Many were decorated; all were unique. Some came by fax, and we set up art supplies to color them. We made copies of everything, so I have these in a big scrapbook. They are marvelous, funny, loving, beautiful.

I lined the box bottom with new Martha Stewart pillows and an old quilt with sentimental history for both of us. I made a little sheet of doggy print flannel. Joan asked to see the casket, which we called the journey box, on Friday afternoon. We brought it out into the yard, and walked her out on the porch. She told us, in her last full sentence, that she loved her box. You know, I am sure this sounds like fantasy. I cannot really convey how it all happened, how we did it. She was so clearly leaving . . . and I was clearly functional in this reality, hyperfunctional I guess, but at the same time I was very much not in this world.

At some point I was lying beside her, holding her. I told her I felt like I was just going to go with her, that I wanted to and couldn't imagine not. She said I should just come on, she could not imagine going on without me either. Then we were just breathing together, and I realized I could no longer match the erratic pattern of her breath. I knew then I was just the midwife, Ninshubur to her Inanna.

She went very gently, a seemingly perceptible shrinking as her spirit left her body. It was about 9:00 p.m. So we moved her to the porch and lit a lot of candles. Some of us sat up awhile telling stories. My son put himself next to the casket. He remembered Joan staying up until the wee hours of the morning on that porch, waiting for him to get home, and it seemed right to him to be there for her.

The next morning, we gathered again. A friend came to play the bagpipes. Constance had decorated her truck camper with evergreens and weeds, bones and feathers. I opened the casket there on the porch to look at her. Her skin was almost translucent, the color of a porcelain doll, her eyelashes inky dark. She held a little stuffed dog that Christy had given her when she was first diagnosed.

We put Joan's box in the camper shell and drove through the bright sunshine to the funeral home. Once there, we took the casket out. Part of the ritual we did there on the side lawn of the funeral involved cutting a string that went from Joan's wrist to mine. I kept that string on my wrist for many months, adding a new piece of embroidery floss for each day.

The memorial service was the next Sunday. Almost four hundred people came. We used both Unitarian-Universalist and pagan rituals, with a smattering of Quaker. Joan's wish was that there be good music, good food, no mention of heaven or Jesus, and dancing. We began by inviting all who had ever been in chorus to come up and join in a sing-along or some chorus greatest hits. This turned out to be some forty women. At the end, we played a tape of Adrianna singing "Somewhere Over the Rainbow," recorded in the studio earlier that week. The ushers passed the baskets of origami bluebirds.

Joan certainly had a very nontraditional service. So did Randi.

Even for her funeral, Randi had insisted that, instead of a traditional funeral service, they have a picnic in her honor and celebrate life. "I hate to think of all of you sitting in some dark room somewhere being sad," she told us. "Go out in the woods and have a picnic. Celebrate my life." And we did.

She died in the first part of March, on the night that the wind shifted, bringing balmy weather for the following week. The picnic was attended by me, her three children and their families, close friends, and their children. We met in a forest preserve, ate, hiked, sang, danced, scattered flowers in the river, cried, and laughed.

Although there was a more traditional service for Caroline than either Joan or Randi had, Anna Marie wrote more about the support she received from friends and family than about the service itself:

> We had the funeral. A lot of the people she worked with came. And a lot of our friends. I can't say the funeral was nice, because to me funerals are not nice. I do not like them.
>
> My mother came to the funeral. My brother and sister. They were not as much support to me as my friends. But I think that is because they know, because they are lesbians or gay guys. They understand more of what you are going through. After the funeral, we went to the church. They had the dinner, whatever you call that, in the basement of their church, which was nice. Then all my gay friends came back to the house and sat there with me. It was good to have the support, but still it is a very lonesome, lonesome feeling.
>
> I went to the church there every Sunday and then after church, I would go to the cemetery. I did that for probably about six months or so. Maybe longer than that. It is funny because I was always in a fog. Eventually I stopped going because it did not help.

RELIGIOUS AND NONRELIGIOUS SERVICES

Anna Marie and Caroline had not been religious during their time together, but Anna Marie found some comfort in attending church in the months after Caroline's death. I did too. I would find it comforting just to sit in the pew and quietly cry through the service. This went on for about six months. It was the quiet, the meditation time, and the sense of a healing presence that spoke to me during those months at church.

Similar to Anna Marie and Caroline, Rose said that she and Steph were not religious, but she arranged for an MCC minister to conduct the memorial service. Rose explained,

> Steph had always planned to be cremated, and that was done. A small memorial service was held in Florida since Steph's brother was still there. Early in January, I organized a memorial service for her here where we had lived together. She had spent

almost all her life in this area, so many local friends and family were able to attend. Although neither of us was religious, we had spent a delightful day at the 1993 March on Washington with a local MCC minister, and he well remembered Steph. He agreed to "officiate" at the informal gathering.

We had a display of pictures of Steph, some of her favorite music, and anyone who wanted was welcome to share memories of her. I do not remember much of the specifics of the service, but I do remember being determined that I (despite my natural reserve) would speak to the gathering about our time together. I did not prepare a speech, but spoke from my heart. I do not know what I said, other than that we were soul mates.

Rose had been determined to speak at Steph's memorial service, while Cassie wanted to sing at Fran's.

When people got up to say something about her, I wanted to sing good-bye to my cherished Fran. At the viewing I sang "Ya No Estas Mas a Mi Lado" (You Are No Longer by My Side). At her graveside, I sang Laura Nyro's "I'm Not Scared of Dying" in front of God and everyone, just for my cherished Fran. I wore the white dress I had been saving for the day when Fran and I would be married.

Although Rose was determined to speak at Steph's funeral and Cassie sang at Fran's, Pat wrote that, like me, she knew she would not be able to speak at Betty's service:

The memorial service was held the following Saturday. Although we had no religious affiliation, I was able to arrange for a lesbian minister to conduct the service. As she had lost a partner herself, she was particularly able to illuminate the enormity of the loss to me for those in attendance. I prepared a statement that a friend read for me; there was no way that I could have stood up to speak.

Several people from the diverse areas of Betty's life spoke of how much they admired her and had enjoyed knowing her. The final gentleman to speak was her former supervisor at work. He said that he had often wondered how she had made it through all that she had, but now he understood the love and support that kept her going in the face of adversity. For the first time he saw the real Betty, the whole Betty.

In Pat's recounting of the memorial service, she conveyed a feeling of satisfaction in having Betty's boss finally understand that Betty was a lesbian. Nora related how friends and family joined her to honor Anne's passing:

> After Anne was gone, the hospice nurse asked me what my relationship with Anne was; I supposed she had been puzzled over the weeks. I answered without hesitation, "She was my lover." Anne's closest friends, the Poker Girls, a group with whom she had played poker for fifteen years, organized the memorial service, held on Halloween. Many of her friends spoke movingly of their relationships with Anne over the years. She was a woman who was deeply loved and respected for her intelligence, her humor, and her modesty. She never boasted about her numerous accomplishments.

The way that Pat described the service for Anne gives a clear picture of the love those in attendance felt for Anne. In Vera's story of Nancy's funeral, there is a sense of celebration and laughter in the midst of the pain.

> The church was just packed with people from all parts of Nancy's life. It was like old home week for the lesbian community; it was fabulous. I ended up standing by the doors and greeting people when they came in, hugging them and saying hello. So there were a million lesbians and other people that I knew from around town or that Nancy knew from our book club and just a variety of other people, including a lot of people from the sight center and a number of Nancy's clients over the years. It was an amazing gathering of folks from all parts of her life.
> The memorial service included some music and some poems, and the minister said really wonderful things, sort of pulling the poems together with other things I had told her about Nancy. And then, as in our union ceremony, I wanted to leave time for people to talk.
> People got up and just told fabulous, funny, wonderful stories—clients, ex-clients, co-workers, and her family. A number

of people told me afterward that her family never got what a wonderful person she was. Someone told me afterward that Nancy's sister was crying outside and said that she was cheated because she never knew her sister. On one hand I was sympathetic, but on the other hand I thought, *Why the fuck not?* They just did not take her seriously.

Finally the minister laughingly said, "I think we have to go eat dinner now." But my favorite part was to end the service with Nancy's favorite song, "Gloria" by Laura Branigan. I stood up and thanked everybody. I told them that I was really moved and touched. I said, "For those of you who knew Nancy, there was not a single song we could have played that would have been more meaningful than this." Then I said, "Hit it, Colleen." And Colleen started playing "Gloria." Everybody who knew Nancy started laughing and it was just fabulous. During dinner we had disco tapes on, which was very, very fun. About 120 people stayed for dinner. Every single person whom I have talked to since said that it was one of the best, most meaningful services they have ever gone to.

Although Nancy's funeral service had a party atmosphere, Pam found the service for Sandy to be deeply moving. She was acknowledged as Sandy's widow by the funeral home, synagogue, friends, and family.

The local Jewish funeral home was called, and they came and got her body. The staff at the funeral home was very respectful of me. I was treated as Sandy's spouse and next of kin. I remember going to the funeral home with our dear friend, Miriam. Sandy wanted a traditional Jewish funeral: a pine casket with no metal parts, a muslin burial shroud and no embalming or preserving at all. We had purchased burial plots through our synagogue several months earlier.

I do not remember much about the funeral, but the chapel at our synagogue was filled to overflowing with friends and family and clients and colleagues. Sandy's son spoke, but I have no idea what he said. We went to the cemetery and I remember just standing there and watching the casket go into the ground. But I felt like I was not really there. I was handed a shovel and placed the first shovelful of earth on top of her casket, followed by family and friends.

The service for Sandy honored both Sandy's wishes and Sandy and Pam's relationship. Marilyn, however, needed to arrange two different services, one for the few who respected that Cheryl was in a lesbian relationship with Marilyn and another for the broader circle of colleagues and acquaintances to whom they had never come out.

I planned the memorial service/funeral with the help of the hospice chaplain and invited only very close family and friends. We held it in the funeral parlor. There was no one there whom my kids did not know by name and sight. The boys and I chose the music. I wrote the eulogy. The hospice chaplain spoke and read from Scripture, and a few friends spoke.

It was warm, and love was palpable in the room. I had planned to have the casket closed after the boys and I had a little time alone, but she looked so beautiful and peaceful we left it open after all. It was a terribly stormy night, and we all agreed it was her protest, but I felt the kids needed this ritual. The burial was just the four of us and eight of our very closest friends. I asked them to come because they were the ones who knew us as a complete family and treated us that way, even though we never talked about it.

A month and a half later we had a formal memorial service where we invited colleagues, friends, Special Olympics folks, students, etc. We had music and speakers and refreshments and spoke of the many wonderful things Cheryl accomplished in her life and all that she had done for the kids she worked with. It was in the library at the university where we worked. It was really very nice. Everyone referred to her tenacity and love.

RITES OF PASSAGE

Funerals and memorial services are rituals, rites of passage that allow us to function during a time when we are confused and disoriented. Lois wrote about the sense of not being fully present as Joan was dying. Rose admitted she did not remember the details of what she said at the funeral, and Pam talked about feeling like she was not really there. Anna Marie said she was walking around in a fog. Ellen described it as being another person for the week.

The widows in this book had a wide variety of experiences regarding funerals and memorials. Those who were out and had the support of family and friends tended to have funerals that were very meaningful to those involved. Some chose more traditional services while others created unique ones. Those who were either not out to or not accepted by family members tended to have negative experiences with funerals and memorial services. Some widows then created their own private memorial services to counteract those feelings.

And then there were those who felt hurt and betrayed by fellow lesbians. Since all of those who died and were widowed in this book were much younger than what one would expect, the youth of their lesbian friends may have been a disadvantage. Too young to expect to be a widow, too young to find others in one's age group who could relate. Another purpose of funerals is to provide a place and time for friends and family to offer support. Sadly, this was lacking in some cases.

No one who has a story in this book talked directly about their religious beliefs, although a few made a point of saying that they were not religious. And yet there certainly seems to be a theme of a sense of spirituality in these lesbians' lives. Even if they did not attend church, they found ministers to conduct the funeral services. It may be that, having been raised in a homophobic religious tradition, they felt forced to leave the church because their sexual orientation was not accepted. I know that some lesbians and gays have found reassurance in the MCC churches. The Jewish lesbians in this study found solace in their Jewish roots. I found a home in Unitarian-Universalism. Some, like Lois, drew on a variety of traditions, including pagan rituals, for comfort. And some have stayed in established churches. It appears that the majority of lesbian widows in this book were not active church attendees, but that did not mean that they were not deeply spiritual women at heart.

Chapter 8

Grief Work

In the months following our life partner's death, we experienced a plethora of emotions: anger, fear, loneliness, guilt, and confusion, to name a few. We may have felt these emotions in our lives before our spouse died, but now their intensity was greater than anything we had previously known. Grief counselors tell us that what we need to do to heal is face the pain, not run from it. This is what is called grief work. In the following section, I describe some of the emotional pain that we experienced. Then I take a look at other experiences we had within the first few months of grieving.

THE PAIN OF GRIEF WORK

One emotion I continued to experience after Emily died was a sense of disbelief. I still had days when I felt like I must be living a nightmare, times when I experienced a sense of unreality. Irene described her internal experience of unreality as a drama taking place in her head:

I felt like three parts of my being were in constant battle. A dark apparition that said I would never get through this, a panicked helpless child that blamed me and begged me to find her, and the rational side of me that did nothing about the other two, just sat motionless and wordless, deserting me in my hour of deepest need. I felt that my very heart had left me, that there was nothing to carry on with.

When I was alone, it was as if I did not exist. I remember nothing of it but the ranting of the two and the unbearable silence of the third. It was like watching a bad play you know will never end. The theater is locked, and the lights on the three on stage never go out. From the moment your eyes open in the early morning hours until you force them shut at night, the ridiculous tragic drama goes on. My dreams were of her suffering and nothing else.

Although I felt a continued sense of being in a nightmare and Pat had a melodrama playing out in her head, Beverly shared how unreal Virginia's death still seemed to her five months later:

> The fourth and fifth months after Virginia's death have had some of the hardest moments because it has seemed more real that she is really never going to be here again. Virginia and I had talked about the fact that she would be gone one day and I would be here. Even though we talked about it quite a lot, I would say sometimes, "You know, even though we are talking like this, I just really cannot believe that it is really going to happen." And I think that is what it was like after she was gone.

Beverly's experience was common. Reality was so jarring to us that we felt disoriented. In addition, we felt a great deal of pain. Rose used the metaphor of feeling like she had an open wound to describe what she was feeling:

> After the funeral, mostly I just concentrated on getting through each day. I remember my continued amazement that I could hurt so much on the inside and yet have no horrible, gaping visible wounds. Even breathing seemed to hurt, and thinking was out of the question. At three months, my grief was still overwhelming and excruciating. I simply survived.

Accepting the reality of our partner's death involved not just an intellectual understanding but an emotional one. It is not unusual to go back and forth between denial and reality at first. Gradually, though, reality sets in.

In the months following Emily's death, I discovered that the slightest thing could trigger tears. My eye catching a piece of jewelry that Em had given me. Walking through a store where we used to shop. Singing a hymn that had been a favorite of Em's. Nora wrote that "small things would trigger fits of weeping" for her in the months following Anne's death. These kinds of moments are called grief spasms. A grief spasm is "an acute upsurge of grief that occurs suddenly and often when least expected. It interrupts your ongoing activities and temporarily leaves you feeling out of control" (Rando, 1988, p. 25).

I would be doing fine one minute and then, wham, I would be in tears. When conflicts arose at work, I would ride home thinking about how I would tell Emily about it, and then remember that she would not be there. Then I would cry. I still occasionally have a grief spasm, but it is not an everyday occurrence as it was right after Emily's death. In my journal at that time I wrote,

I wonder how long it will take before I have a day where I do not cry about Em. I spent my first couple hours this morning cleaning the apartment. I cried through much of it, the deep sobbing cry I had before she died, the deep sobbing I would experience when I would think of life without her. When this happens, it feels like I will never stop crying and never be able to function. But I do stop. And I do go on.

Janet related how sad she felt after Chris's death. She also commented on how difficult it was to lose one's life partner:

There were no happy times and no laughter for a once cockeyed optimist. This was hard for me even to admit. Somewhere along the way, someone said it is okay to lose a child, and we expect to lose parents, but to lose a partner/spouse, you never fully recover. I guess this is true, at least for me.

Janet's observation that you never fully recover from losing a partner was a truth that all of us who were widowed discovered. Over time and with support we might hurt less, but the loss of our spouse was a life-altering experience that will affect us for the rest of our lives. Tears and sadness, however, were not the only emotions we experienced in the months after our partner passed away. Nora voiced the kind of anger we all felt.

I was still experiencing the pain of my son's death too. I felt a great deal of rage. When a convicted child murderer was going to be executed in New Mexico I felt a sense of injustice. How should someone who committed something so heinous have a better chance at life than a brilliant woman and an innocent child?

Since all of us in this book were widowed at a young age and our partner died too young, questioning the injustice of this happening was a feeling we all grappled with. In addition to disbelief, sadness, and anger, another emotion many of us whose partner suffered for a time felt was relief. I was relieved for Emily, glad that she would no longer be in pain. But I was also relieved for myself. I no longer had to do any more caretaking, and I also did not have to deal with the conflicts in our relationship any longer. Although I felt guilty for thinking these things, that was how I honestly felt, right along with deeply mourning Em's death. Both the relief and the guilt are considered normal reactions to loss. Dale, who had spent seven years going back and forth to a nursing home to take care of Carol, shared her sense of relief after Carol's death:

> Right after she died there was a sense of relief, but I did not know what to do with myself. I was so used to stopping by the nursing home during the day. It was a strange time. I was involved with other women while Carol was in the nursing home and right before she went in. The relationships never lasted in part because I was never able to really leave Carol. It generated some hostility—my need to see Carol every day to make sure she was all right.

Although certainly a nontraditional situation, I think Dale's experience is a good example of the depth of emotional attachment in lesbian relationships. Even though she was involved with other women, Dale was still deeply bound to Carol. Although she did not use this word to describe their relationship, it seems to me that we might call Dale and Carol soul mates. And a soul mate connection is not easily broken.

Another feeling we experienced as widows was loneliness, but we had different ways of dealing with it. During that first year after Emily's death, I spent a lot of time alone, by choice. It was all I could do to function at work. I did not have the energy to socialize. I think my friends felt that they had lost both Emily *and* me. Many other widows also withdrew and isolated themselves for a period of time. We were lonely, and yet we could not bear to be around people. Ellen wrote,

> At first, I did not want to talk to anybody or do anything with anybody. I just wanted to be alone. It was months before I

wanted to be around people. Every day I would go to the cemetery and be with her. I lit a candle every night and said prayers
for Kate. I talked with a therapist every week in the winter. In the
spring I started feeling better, but then it got much worse at
around six months. Then I started working with a spiritual director. Things that did not make any sense to me, he helped me find
words for the experience. I was so incredibly lonely during this
time.

Ellen spoke of her loneliness and how her pain eased and then
came back again. That is the cyclic nature of grief. Anita, too, was
lonely, but she also continued to be in shock over Holly's death.

At three months I was still grieving. I tried to do things but I
could not. I just isolated myself. I thought that since Holly was
much younger than me, that she would outlive me. But you cannot count on age. It does not mean a thing. You cannot even
count on health; she died unexpectedly, which took me for a
loop. I just did not believe it. I have many things of hers in each
room of my house that provide me with solace.

Like me, Anita found that she just did not have the energy to be social in those early months. In Holly's absence, Anita took comfort in
possessions that reminded her of Holly. Vera also spent time alone but
shared something she did that was both painful and meaningful:

I spent a lot of time alone. I spent time with friends, watched
TV, read, walked my little dog and just . . . was. That was really a
good thing. Over the course of the summer, I redid my will. It
felt important to have it done, but it was just so sad.

One of the most meaningful things that I did, but also one of
the saddest, was dealing with the rings from our union ceremony. I wanted to do something with the two rings; I wanted
them to be in a different form but together, sort of like our relationship is now, on a spiritual level. I took the two rings to a jew-
eler and had them made into a pendant using the silver the stones
were set in. It was a really sad thing to do but it was also really
great. It looks beautiful and I'm really, really glad to have it.
I wear it all the time. It was a really meaningful thing to do. I
thought of it as a gift.

In the midst of her sorrow, Vera took comfort in the pendant she created with their rings, just as Anita related that she took comfort in possessions of Holly's that she kept. Although some of us preferred to be alone, Nora wrote how, in the months after Anne's death, she sought solace in other women:

> Grief distorts your thinking; you act in totally uncharacteristic ways. My reaction was to run out and find someone whose shoulder I could cry on. Unfortunately these women assumed that I wanted *them*. In retrospect, I think it must have been awful for these women to be with a woman who broke into uncontrollable weeping every now and then.
>
> Then I spent a year on my own. Now I feel that I want to commit to a long-term relationship soon. I do not imagine I will find the peaceful love I had with Anne, but I have a home and a surviving son to care for and raise in the happiest, most stable way I can.

In a similar vein, Lois wrote about wanting someone to have sex with her:

> I really struggled with feeling desperately sexually. I needed so much to be made love to; it was some kind of primal need to feel myself alive and very literally touched. I really tried to get one of my bedtime buddies to do it; she was probably quite right to resist. A very old but distant friend finally did it; she was pretty horrified afterward and has never understood what a huge favor she did me. I have found this subject quite taboo in books on grief, though other widows (and widowers) I have talked to have told me of similar experiences.

Although initially desperate for intimate contact, both Nora and Lois eventually learned to be alone. Rather than a desperate affair, Shirley connected with a new partner less than a year after Terry's death. She e-mailed me nine months after Terry's death:

> I just got back from a week's vacation in Florida. I have found a wonderful woman who is a godsend. She is someone I have been praying for all my life. She recently lost her father from illness and old age. We have been wonderful for each other.

In the months after we were widowed, we experienced a range of emotions including disorientation, sadness, anger, relief, guilt, loneliness, and longing. Grief work involves allowing ourselves to feel those feelings, no matter how painful they are, rather than denying or running away from them or drowning them with alcohol or drugs. This does not happen quickly or easily. One way to think of it is to understand that grief is not an event that happens but a process that we go through over time (Wolfelt, 1992).

HEALTH

Another problem some lesbian widows faced in the first year after their partner's death was their own illness. I was diagnosed with arthritis in my hips while Emily was dying and found it increasingly painful and difficult to walk after she died. I tried different medications and eventually found something that helped, but I have noticed that the arthritis seems to flare up each year around the time of the anniversary of Emily's death.

Although Pat initially ate all the ice cream and cookies she wanted after Betty's death, after about six weeks Pat began changing her diet and exercising.

> I started swimming a couple times a week. As one would expect, with the addition of exercise, my energy level began to increase. After a couple more months I added bicycling and yoga to my exercise regimen. I also changed my diet to more of the vegetarian foods that I like. The result was that, over the next eighteen months, I lost about twenty-five pounds and looked and felt better than I had in fifteen years. For the most part I have kept it off and kept up my exercise regimen.

Unlike Pat, weight gain was not an issue for Beverly. Rather, after years of nursing Virginia and staying healthy, she got a bad cold shortly after Virginia passed away.

> It was almost five months after she was gone before I was able just to sit down and read in the afternoon as we had usually done when she was well. One experience that I have had is that it is not unusual for me, when I am upset or pressured, to get ill. The

three and one-half years she was ill, I was not sick. But two months after she was gone I got a horrible cold that lasted for two weeks, and then I have had four bouts of gastrointestinal problems.

Physical ailments while grieving are a common problem. After Chris died, Janet had a major health crisis when she herself was diagnosed with cancer.

In 1988 my mother was diagnosed with cancer, and I retired from the fire department and took care of her until she died in 1991. Taking all the hard lessons I learned from Chris, I knew just what to do beforehand. All the planning paid off, and I felt so much better in asking the hard questions. And my mother was more at peace with everything. I think the most important thing to learn in life is that it is the *quality* of life, not quantity of life, which is critical.

Just before my mother died, I discovered a lump, which was cancer. I did not share this with her because she already felt guilty for being a burden (which is totally wrong). I have fought it every step of the way. I am a survivor and cancer is an inconvenience, nothing more. It will not get me. Afterward I found a "no brain required" job and excelled. I am a ten-year survivor and walk every year for those whom I have loved and lost to cancer.

Grief affects us in all dimensions of life—physically, emotionally, intellectually, spirituality, socially. We all grieve in our own unique ways and so the particular symptoms may vary. For instance, Vera developed a cold while Janet was diagnosed with cancer; Nora wrote of her anger while I felt a combination of relief and guilt. But whatever the symptoms, we were responding to a loss that had changed our lives forever.

FEELING HER PRESENCE

Another typical experience, especially in the first few months after the death of a loved one, is to have a sense of our deceased partner's presence and to talk to her as if she were still alive. Sometimes other people may wonder about us if we tell them we are doing this, but it is a perfectly normal way to react to our loss.

I made periodic visits to Em's gravesite that first year. It felt to me like she wanted me to just sit there with her for a while, just feel her presence, as if she were missing me too. In fact, through all those early months after Emily's death I would have times when I sensed her presence. These experiences were always affirming and encouraging to me. One time, for example, I was thinking about why this had to happen, why she had to die, and I sensed her telling me to appreciate the time we had together and to know that I gave her what she needed, a sense of being loved. In my journal I wrote,

Although we had talked about being "little old ladies sipping tea and growing old together," it was not meant to be. It was a transition time for both of us; we supported each other through changes in our lives. I was able to accompany her on her journey to death, and she died knowing she was loved. She empowered me to be where I am, who I am today.

In the midst of my grief, I was trying to make sense of the experience. Talking to Em and experiencing her presence helped me do that. Irene shared how she felt a sense of MJ's presence:

Not a day goes by that I do not think of her and speak to her. Somehow, starting from the morning she died, I have the gift of believing she touches me and makes her presence known to me through sunlight. It is an incredible feeling to have that gift, that constant presence. I do not know how it came about. I did not make it up and it has never left me.

I had several dreams about Em during the year after her death. I could not always remember the dream when I awoke, but I always had the intense sense of her presence.

In this dream, Em and I were giving some kind of presentation. Em kept wanting to add this and lengthen that even though I did not think we would have enough time. Finally we had to just end the presentation. The dream seemed so real. Like she was alive and I really had talked to her. Like the presentation in the dream, her life and our relationship had been cut much shorter than we had planned.

Heather shared a dream she had about Ruth:

When Ruth died, I wanted to dream about her. I remember I did not have a single dream about her for the first few months.

When I finally did, I was pleased, and told myself that she had been too busy before that to enter my dreams. Playing basketball, no doubt—something that had been a nice part of her life, but gone well before I ever met her.

Time must be different in the afterlife, so it took several months before the first quarter of her first game ended and she was able to get to a dream booth to pay me a visit. No, I do not really believe any of this. I am agnostic, actually, but the images are very comforting. And I add in various pets as they die also. Ruth riding my current partner's Labrador while dribbling a basketball, or shooting baskets with my cat, Rover, on her shoulders.

Dreaming of our loved one or having a sense of her presence are typical experiences after we lose a loved one. They help us do our grief work at an unconscious level. Even though dreaming about Em or feeling her presence would result in my crying, I still found these times very comforting.

HOME

Losing a partner, for most of us, meant losing the person with whom we shared our home, and that influenced our attitude toward that home in different ways. Although my minister reminded me that it was best to not make major decisions during the first year after a loved one died, I had no choice. I had to physically move out of the house that Emily and I had shared. And, if I had to move, I decided I was going to move closer to work. I did not want to commute an hour if Em was not there to come home to. A few weeks after Emily's death, I found an apartment that seemed ideal, located in a quiet, parklike area on a river. I decided I would create a retreat center and give myself time to grieve and recover before I started thinking about what I was going to do with the rest of my life. I packed and moved.

At the same time I was moving, my brother, sister, and I worked together to care for my mother in the last weeks of her life. I walked through that time and then her funeral in a sort of stupor, too numb from Em's death to fully feel the loss of my mother. I did find, though, that having a place that was my own felt better to me than I think I would have felt continuing to live in the home we had shared. Having my own place helped me develop the sense of creating a new life for myself in the midst of my despair. Janet also found that she could not bear to live in the same house that she had shared with Chris.

> I slept on the couch, as I was not able to go into our bedroom, and quickly came to feel suffocated in the house. Nowhere to run, nowhere to hide, and I knew that no amount of drugs and booze could make me feel again. Soon after the funeral I left the house with very little. I hated all the things which created "our home" and just could not face them. I left and never went back. I had friends give away everything from that life.

Janet's grief led her to leave behind reminders of Chris, whereas Maureen found solace in the home she had shared with Dale.

> After she died, I went back upstairs to our bedroom. I had not been there to sleep for the whole month, and it was so strange for her not to be in the house. Even now I feel her presence here all the time.

Anita took comfort in the things that reminded her of Holly.

> I have many things of hers in each room of my house and that provides me with solace. Looking at the things she gave me, looking at her pictures. I look at the things she gave me like the coffee table book and I look at them with fondness, touch them with fondness. So it is a good memory.

Vera wrote about the positive energy she felt in her home:

> Another thing that I think has been very good for me is that I really love my house and I feel really comfortable here. This house has totally wonderful energy—people comment on it. It is this real peaceful space and I feel safe here. I know when I was going to the hospice group for those few weeks, there was one woman there who could not even go back into her home. There was another woman who was in her house but it just felt awful to her. I am very grateful that I have never had that.

Like Vera, Donna also found comfort in the home she had shared with Randi. In fact, she related that one of the most unhelpful things anybody said to her after Randi's death was to question her continuing to live there.

> "You don't want to rattle around by yourself in that big empty house in the country anymore, so you are planning to move back into the city, aren't you?" I, feisty even in the midst of grief, replied, "That big empty house happens to be my *home.*"

Lois's son moved in with her after Joan's death, helping her to deal with the day-to-day issues of owning a home.

> My children were very protective and my son moved in with me. He was twenty-eight and we had not lived together since he was fourteen. The time together was healing for me. His mere presence provided company, ongoingness. Sometimes my grief behaviors made him crazy, like listening to a Hindu chant over and over again. He kept the physical stuff going, kept the bills paid, took out the trash. A couple of years later he told me how hard it was for him to hear me cry. He did not feel strong enough to be the one to hold me, and later he wished he had tried harder.

The presence of her son and the familiarity of the home she had shared with Joan provided Lois with a sense of the continuity of life. For me, it was not just the apartment that I moved into that provided a place for healing, it was also the solace afforded by nature. When the weather was nice, I took long walks through a park and along the river. I felt like Mother Earth had welcomed me to this particular setting, to hold me as I healed. I would walk along, meditating, and often crying. The living room window in my new apartment had a beautiful view of trees and the river.

> I'm sitting in my living room, looking out the window as it gets dark and the lights come on. The river is beautiful during the day; breathtaking at night. But I can't believe I am here, living alone, and Emily is gone.

In those first few months after Em's death, I sat for hours looking out the window, feeling that the winter outside reflected the winter inside of me. Everything looked dead, but I knew life would eventually come again.

WAYS OF ESCAPE

Grieving is hard work. I escaped it at times by reading novels. I also watched more television during the year after Em's death than I had probably watched in the previous ten years altogether, as if the television were a drug that numbed the pain. Going to work was another way of getting my mind off my grief. For me, working affirmed that I was a person, that I had a life to live even though Emily was gone. Some widows, like me, continued to work. Others, however, were able to not work and felt that not working was therapeutic for them. Joy and Rose were among the workers. Joy wrote,

> I went to school every day and taught vigorously, knowing that this would keep me concentrated on the job. But nights were crying, tossing, turning, and more crying. I wanted no one near me. I could only dwell on the idea of suicide, because everything was wrong and nothing was fair. I had one good lesbian friend in Berlin who called often and Christine would call also. They were the only two people I would talk with.

Joy kept working despite how lonely and desperate she felt at night. Rose shared how painful those early months were for her:

> For the first six months after Steph died, I was in a completely altered state. Each morning I would wake up and there would be a split second of peace before the pain came crashing back. I have never hurt so much in my life, or for such an extended time. To the extent that I thought at all, I remember my continued amazement that I could hurt so much on the inside and yet have no horrible, gaping, visible wounds on the outside.
>
> Even breathing seemed to hurt, and thinking was out of the question. Each day I went to work and came home, did the necessary chores at home and not much else. Everything at home and many things at work reminded me of Steph—her presence in my home is strong to this day.

Joy and Rose worked despite their pain and tears. Pat and Lois were both in a position to not have to work after their partners died. They found that this allowed them a time of healing. Pat related that she needed a few months to recuperate:

I had no concept of the magnitude of grief until I experienced it myself. For months it was as if half of me had been ripped away and I was adrift without direction. I rested for the first couple of months. The last few months of Betty's life, I had just kept moving because I did not dare to stop or I would not have been able to carry on. It felt really good just to stop, flop in the recliner, and watch TV and not move after dinner. My sisters and a close friend kept close tabs on me, always concerned that I might not be eating or sleeping.

After about six weeks, some women I work with asked me to join them in a summer bowling league and I did. I knew that I needed to get out of the house and have some fun at least one day a week, so I did it for the summer.

Although Lois was not employed immediately after Joan's death, she kept busy with projects and activities.

In the immediate time after Joan died, the most helpful thing was that I did not work. I had all the time I needed to just be. I was pretty zombie-like for a while, and I have few memories of those first couple months. I remember watering all the flowers, and rearranging them as the blossoms faded. I went to church and practiced for the holiday singing with the choir, a sort of normal activity. Mostly tears would run down my face all the time.

Later I tore out the kitchen and remodeled it. We had always meant to do it, and just never had. It bothered Joan that she was leaving me with it still to do. It sort of felt like I was showing her I could make it on my own. When I started, I chose a very dull neutral color scheme. By summer when I finished it, it was bright blue, with a cloud ceiling and a sunrise mural over the stove.

Lois found that the months of not working after Joan's death gave her time and space to begin to heal. Heather described how a short break from work helped her.

I was working as a therapist when Ruth died, and I remember feeling glad that Thanksgiving was not too far away. That allowed me a little extra time to get myself together before returning to clinical work. For the first couple of weeks, I could not imagine sitting there for fifty minutes with a client, confident I would not start crying. By the time I came back, I did okay with that.

Vera, like Heather, was able to briefly have a respite from work.

> Because I am a faculty member, I am able to take the summer off. I was scheduled to teach over summer but I woke up one morning and just thought, "I can't." So someone taught my classes for me. That was the best thing that I did. I was not sure how it would be to have so much time off without Nancy. I had taken summers off in the past but she had always come home at the end of the day. It ended up being fine.

Shirley thought that keeping busy in the months right after her partner's death helped her. Like Joan, she too undertook a remodeling project.

> I have found that keeping myself busy is a big help to me. Terry and I had started to remodel our home before she died, so I am continuing on with that project. I have finished two bedrooms in the last six months and am getting ready to start on my own bedroom. That will be more difficult because everything in there is "Terry and me." I do not know what to do with everything. I certainly do not want to get rid of it, but do not think I want everything to remain in there either. I want to make it *my* room now instead of *our* room.

Keeping busy with remodeling helped Shirley, but she was also faced with the quandary of wanting to remodel to make the bedroom her own and yet not wanting to give up Terry's presence in the room either. Beverly wondered if something was wrong with her because she needed to get out of the house and do other things.

> About two months after Virginia was gone, I met a lesbian who had lost her partner a couple of years ago. She had not gone out of their home except to the grocery store and the drug store for seven months. I was just the opposite. I could not stay home all day. I felt compelled to go out and do all the things we had talked of doing: going to the movies we had talked about, eating at the

restaurants. And even though I know everybody's experience is different, I was wondering, Is something wrong with me? Am I missing something as I tried to go through this grieving process?

All of the widows in this book were in mourning in the months after their partner's passing, but all did it in slightly different ways. There is no one right way or wrong way to grieve. There is just your way.

COMING OUT

Another thing that happened in my life during the months following Emily's death was that I realized that my new life, whatever it might look like in the future, needed to involve being out, completely out. This had been one of the most frequent and painful disagreements I had with Emily over the years. I wanted to come out and she did not. She believed that my being out would out her. After her death, however, the pain that I felt inside was too incredible to keep to myself.

I have learned that it makes an internal difference for me whether I tell someone I have lost my best friend or my partner. Saying that my best friend died just does not do it for me anymore. It minimizes my pain and our relationship. I cannot go on living in the closet anymore.

I went with friends to the National Women's Music Festival eight months after Emily's death. Afterward, I wrote the following in my journal:

I had a nice mix of alone time, companionship, and community here. Mainly, I guess, I am leaving here today with a sense of being part of this community in a way I have not felt before. I am doing and becoming everything that Em was afraid of and that she held me back from [being an out lesbian]. This is why her death is such a mixed blessing. She was my soul mate at one level but her fears and caution controlled us.

I came out to my brother and sister, both of whom were surprisingly supportive. I started coming out to faculty in my department one at a time, and later to my students. And as I made new friends, I told them that my partner had recently passed away and I identified myself as a widow. Marilyn decided that she too needed to come out.

For thirty-one years we lived and loved in the closet. Not a very healthy thing to do, in retrospect, but there were many reasons for it at the time. But as Cheryl lay there dying, I needed to come out. I needed someone to understand that this was not my good friend who was dying. I needed my grief to be understood and so I came out to the social worker and chaplain from hospice. I needed to validate our love. They helped me to do that in the short weeks they worked with us as a family and in the months later that they worked with me. Gradually I came out to close friends and then eventually to just about everyone. I feel badly that she never let herself tell anyone of our love, but by the time I was ready, Cheryl was dealing with dying and I guess it was just too much.

After the death of a life partner, we experienced emotional pain like nothing we had ever experienced before. In that way, our grief was no different from a married widow's experience of grief. The issue of whether we were out or not, however, was a factor in how others responded to us and how we felt about ourselves. The majority of lesbian widows who have shared their experience in this chapter were out and they tended to be treated as grieving widows by friends and family. Marilyn and I, on the other hand, experienced the pain of not having our loss acknowledged as the loss of a spouse until we made the decision to come out. Only then did we feel validated instead of invisible. Other lesbian widows, unable to come out for fear of losing their jobs, remained invisible.

Chapter 9

Comfort and Support

In our sorrow, we found comfort where we could—from friends, family, pets, our home, wherever and whoever could ease the pain. Friends were the main source of support for the majority of lesbian widows.

FRIENDS

I was fortunate to receive a great deal of support from friends. For the first few months after Emily's death, they called, visited, took me to lunch or dinner. Their support was critical because my family was preoccupied with my mother's death and taking care of my father.

Ellen related how listening friends helped her with her grief:

> There was one couple, friends of Kate, who just *showed up* every week after the funeral. One or the other would call me, and sometimes we went out to eat. It was incredible. I did not know them, but they were present with me for about four months. I think back on that with such gratitude. They just listened. Just that consistency was incredible, every week without fail. And they did not say anything or get in the way. It was such an unusual quality.

In our culture, people often feel awkward around widows because they do not know what to say. These friends of Kate's did not have to say anything. It was their presence that was comforting. Jane shared how two of her friends provided a shoulder for her to cry on:

> I floundered about for months. My friend Bill, who had lost his partner to AIDS, was always willing to talk with me. He listened

to me often and saw me cry many times. Our friend Ann called about every four or five days, especially at first.

Bill knew, from his own experience, how painful it was for Jane to lose her partner. He also knew that listening and allowing her to cry were the best way to support her. Traci was very clear about how important the support of her friends was to her. "My friends all told me that I was the only one they knew who had never been in therapy for anything, and that I should go. I told them I did not need therapy. My friends were my therapy."

Lois also had a strong friendship network of support.

I cannot imagine surviving without this kind of support: A couple friends were willing to come and stay with me until I fell asleep several nights a week. Deb was particularly wonderful about this. She would lay down with me and hold me tight. Most of the time I would cry; sometimes I would just fall asleep right after, and sometimes we would talk and giggle. I wanted her to make love to me, but she was able to resist that without, remarkably, running away.

Also very high on the list would be the care team. We all stayed in touch. One month after Joan's death, we had a weekend retreat. I designed a couple of activities (I am a trainer by profession) for us. In one we constructed a timeline of the last week of Joan's time. I put up a flip chart page for each day, and everyone wrote memories of that day—what they did and observed—on Post-it notes and stuck them to the appropriate page. Then we read them all over as a group. It was very cathartic, and it served to fill in gaps that we either did not have memory of, or were not around for, or did not have time to share when it was all happening.

On Sunday morning we spent hours making collages loosely based on the questions "Where are you now?" and "How are you changed?" We were all sort of amazed at how long this took. When we were all done, we each talked about what we had depicted. I recently listened to the audiotape of this session, and the depth of intimacy is simply breathtaking.

Lois reaped the benefits of being part of a community of strong women. Even in their grief, they worked together to bring solace to one another. Pam was overwhelmed with the support she received from family, friends, and clergy as well as her therapist.

> I received so much support from friends and family (except my own), as well as the rabbis at the synagogue, members of other faith communities, as well as my incredibly wonderful and awesome therapist. Andy and I have worked together for seventeen years now, and she was with me from the giddy beginning of this relationship to the painful end and beyond. She saved my life. Boo the dog was also a great help.
>
> Sandy's business partner has been a wonderful support. We have stayed in touch and speak on a regular basis. I am the primary dog sitter for her dogs. Our friend Grace was also a big help. Other friends called and sent cards. Sandy's clients, who for the most part knew who I was, were warm and very respectful. The local lesbian chorus sent a lovely note and planted a tree in Israel in Sandy's name. Sandy had done work with the chorus to help them iron out some wrinkles several years before she got sick.
>
> Sandy's friend, Mary, would call or just stop by to see me all the time. She took me to lunch and had me to dinner at her house. Mary's husband, Al, is also a dear friend. Mary and Al's daughter, Lisa, and her husband, Carlos, always joined us. They now have a son, Henry, and another baby on the way. Sandy would have loved Henry.

Similar to the kind of support Joan received, Pam had a circle of friends and family sustaining her in the months after Sandy's death. Nora wrote more about what people did that felt supportive to her than about the quantity of help she received.

> Most helpful were the people who did practical things for me, even simple things like shopping, helping me take care of my son. This was because I was so overwhelmed much of the time. I needed someone to take care of *me* because I had exhausted all my resources taking care of others.

Beverly noted that the friends who had supported her through Virginia's illness were now also the friends who nurtured her afterward.

After the funeral, family and friends were very helpful with their support, by letting me tell them about the day she died, about how much I miss her, and about how I was feeling. Actually, the support I got from family and friends was a continuation of the support they had given me the entire three and a half years that Virginia was sick. They never failed to ask how I was feeling. It was immensely helpful for them to acknowledge the responsibility I had as her caretaker and the huge loss I experienced at her passing.

What a difference it made to Beverly to have family and friends who could acknowledge what she had gone through, who listened to her and asked how she was feeling. In this sense, Beverly's grief was not invisible but rather validated, perhaps not in the larger society, but certainly within her own support network. Vera also was comforted by close friends, but she noted that, despite their support, none of them had been widowed and none of them really knew what she was going through.

My friends are great. I have six to eight really close friends. A number of people told me after Nancy died that I could call them in the middle of the night because I had no idea if I would have trouble sleeping. I did not though. My friends are all really wonderful and they will listen, depending on who they are. I have one friend who I love but whenever I am going through a hard time she will say, "But you are okay." She seems to need to know that I am okay, whatever okay means.

I asked my friends to please continue to invite me to things even if I do not go, and they really have been very consistent. I know they love me a lot and I love them a lot. But they have not gone through this. None of them have gone through anything like this, and the sad fact of the matter is that a lot of the time I am alone. I have spent quite a bit of time alone and most of the time that feels okay, but sometimes it does not. When it does not, really what it means is that I am missing Nancy a lot.

Vera let her friends know that, even though she was spending a lot of time alone, they should not give up on her. Irene commented that she learned to allow others to support her. As lesbians, we may be strong, relatively independent women, but this is one time in our lives when we need to let others help us.

> I had many friends and family reach out to help me. I took them up on every offer to be with them. "Letting" my friends and family reach me and support me in my grief was one of the things that helped me most. I tried not to close up even though I wanted to. I tried to let the love they offered reach me in my despair.

Irene knew that, even in her sorrow, her friends were there for her. For Joy and Lois, it was even a step beyond that. They shared how the support they received from friends kept them from committing suicide. Joy explained,

> In May, Christine called and wrote trying to get me to commit to coming to the Golden Threads ceremony, saying that she needed to see me and have me with her and that it would be helpful for me. I told her no, as I preferred to be alone. I was still thinking of suicide although I never mentioned it to anyone. At the last possible moment in June, I decided to fly to P'town to retrace Barbara's and my steps, our bike rides . . . every path we had taken there together. Christine was grateful I was there and listened to me break down again with my story.
>
> I participated in the celebration politely, but stayed on to refresh my mind with every step that Barbara and I had taken in this town. I suffered intensively every night after each day's journey of retraced memories. This obviously is what made me decide to return to Germany and get a gun to kill myself.
>
> The day of my return to Germany, my Berlin friend phoned and said that she had a week's vacation and wanted to come to visit with me. I was reluctant, but said she could. When she arrived, she asked questions, listened, asked more questions and listened, insisted that we go out and attend the city's gay parade and do many other things constantly. But she kept listening and reminding me of how good it is to get everything out, how she cared, how she knew it would take a long painful time for me and how she would be there for me anytime, but that I must start thinking about the flowers and sunlight and life again if even ever so slowly. After she left, I slowly gave up the suicidal thoughts. The night crying continued throughout the year, however.

Lois did not have a plan for terminating her life, but she did experience suicidal thoughts for a time.

> Three months after Joan's death I was barely functional. I think I had the most suicidal ideation in late spring, about six months after. It was the anniversary of her initial diagnosis, then of her best time the following year, followed quickly by more metastasis.
>
> I was asked to join a new work group at church, a group that would be a most significant support over the next year because, while they honored my loss, they also saw me as a useful human despite that.

Joan's comment that her church work group saw her as a useful human being is similar to what I gained by continuing to teach. By maintaining myself professionally, I held onto a sense of myself as a person. I was not just a widow. I had colleagues who respected me, and that helped me feel good about myself at a time when I otherwise felt pretty miserable.

Heather wrote that she did not want to talk to a therapist who did not know Ruth about Ruth. She turned to her friends for support because they knew Ruth and could understand what Heather had been through.

> I was a clinical psychology student when Ruth died, and am a psychologist now. I have not done most of the things we often recommend for people who are grieving. I did not go to a bereavement support group, did not read about it, did not write her a "good-bye" letter, have not seen a therapist since she died. I just wanted to talk to others who cared about Ruth.

In this section, I have shared the many different ways that friends supported us in our grief. Anita stated very succinctly how her friends and family helped her. "How did my family and friends support me? By just being there. Just being there."

In contrast to married widows, lesbians tend to find more support from friends than family. For many lesbians, friends have become family, especially if they have been rejected by their biological families. Sadly, though, some lesbians felt a lack of support from their lesbian friends. Samantha, for example, was disappointed by how she was treated, although she also recognized that she may have played a role by not asking for help.

> I think that the lack of support from the women's community surrounded and deeply affected my ability to trust. Unfortunately, I also know myself well enough to know that I have a hard time asking for the support when I probably need it most. I am learning to forgive and that has felt better than harboring the anger and the hurt.

Although Samantha was hurt by friends, Nora was wounded when Anne's former lover took over and did not acknowledge Nora as Anne's widow.

> In the days that followed Anne's funeral, Anne's previous partner took over the distribution of her things. I felt as though my relationship with Anne was of no account, as though her former partner was the wife and I was some trifling mistress. I was deeply upset about this because Anne had told me so many stories about the way her former partner constantly put her down during their years together. I thought Anne would have turned in her grave at the way she took control of everything.

The insensitivity of lesbians to the pain of the lesbian widow invalidated the relationship as well as the loss of the survivor. Grief specialists stress the importance of receiving support in the grief recovery process. Lack of support makes grieving more difficult, if not impossible. In a sense, lesbian widows who did not receive support from lesbian friends were doubly invalidated, first by society in general and second by the lesbian community in particular.

FAMILY SUPPORT

Some lesbian widows received no support from their families, while others received care from family members that was a major support in their healing. Donna, for example, felt close to Randi's children, whereas Maureen was shunned by Robin's family. Rose said her family was too far away to be of much support, while Lois's children rallied around her. Anita wrote this about her family:

I was out but Holly was not. But I think that if I was heterosexual, I would have gotten more support. My family probably would have openly talked about Holly. They did not. They knew I was grieving and they supported me, but I could not talk about how much I missed her, what she did for me, what I did for her. I could not talk about anything like that. Even though I was out, it was not an exchange of conversation like husbands and wives do and when a husband dies or a wife dies. They can talk about everything. I could not do that. I knew my boundaries. I knew my limitations.

Although she received minimal support from her family, Anita received outright hostility and rejection from Holly's brother.

I never was allowed in her home after she died. Never had that opportunity. When Holly was alive and I went to her home, I painted there, I did the lawn, I shoveled snow, I pruned the bushes. I mean I cleaned house, I did dishes, cooked over there and did laundry, ironing. The day after she died, that was it. I was never in her house again. Her freaking brother. How could anyone be so mean? My god, he thought he was punishing me. He thought that if he could control and possess everything she had, he won.

If Anita and Holly had been able to legally marry, Holly's brother could not have walked in and taken over. Although Pam did not receive the outright hostility that Anita did from her partner's family, she experienced a great deal of pain over the lack of support from her own family. This was intensified when her mother died two weeks after Sandy passed away.

Sandy and I were both "out." She was one of the first openly lesbian psychotherapists in the community. We were involved in the Jewish and gay communities as well as the Jewish gay and lesbian movement. We had planned to spend the rest of our lives together, which we did.

Early on in our relationship, I told my mother that I had in fact "met a nice Jewish doctor." She did not see the humor in that right away. My mother could never deal with the fact that I am a lesbian. She never spoke about it to me after I came out to her and to the best of my knowledge never spoke to her sisters or my grandmother about me. I was happily out to all of them. I tried to accept my mother's limitations as best I could. But it did and still does cause me pain.

About two weeks after Sandy's death, I got a call from my father telling me it was time to go back to Texas; my mother was dying. My mother was in hospice and was comatose when I got there. We all stayed with her, held her hand and talked to her. We waited three days and just before we got to the hospice on the fourth day, my mother passed away.

We had a memorial service for friends who lived there. A family memorial service was to be held several weeks later in Florida. I did not go to the Florida service. I know my family did not understand, but I was too wiped out and frankly too angry with my family to go. Because my immediate family was so caught up in my mother's illness, I got little or no support from them while I was also trying to deal with Sandy's illness and death.

While Pam was hurt by her family's lack of support, Lois, in contrast, shared this delightful story about her granddaughter.

My granddaughter was in some ways the best support, because she just needed me to be her granny, because she was not afraid to talk about and have feelings about Joan. She has combined her knowledge of Christian practice with the pagan practices she's seen at my house, and made her own path.

Not long after Joan died, we went for a walk and picked up sweet gum seed pods, those spiky balls. When we got home, she asked if I wanted to pray to Grandma Joan with her. "You just talk into the gum ball, and then throw it up and she will catch it," she told me. "You first." I was somewhat overcome, but with my lips to the gum ball, I managed to say a few things, then handed off the gum ball to her. "Well, I have a lot more to say than that," she said. After a long narrative about how she was, how all the animals were, and how much she missed Joan, she kissed the gum ball, then climbed to the porch rail and heaved it with all her might into the air.

In a time of great pain for Lois, her granddaughter provided her with a sweet reminder of innocence. In a similar vein, Ellen related a tender story about her parents. Expecting rejection, she received their acceptance and support instead.

> My parents never accepted Kate as my partner. I was not cut off but we were not welcome to stay in their house. But when Kate died, my parents were waiting for me when I got back from Hawaii with open arms. All my mother could say was, "How can you ever forgive me? I am so sorry."

In contrast to Ellen's parents, Janet's family had accepted Chris as their daughter-in-law almost from the beginning, and they grieved along with Janet when Chris died.

> Chris loved my mother and my mother loved her. Chris loved her new family and discovered how much fun holidays could be. All the while we made lots of great memories. Thinking back and looking at it today, it must be very cold for those who do not have warm loving memories to hold dear. I am one of the lucky ones.

In their answers to my questionnaire, only eleven widows stated explicitly that they had the support of their families. All eleven were out to their families.

ONLINE SUPPORT

Something else I tried in an effort to address my pain was an online widow chat group. But I got off almost immediately because it seemed to be mainly men whining about the housework and child care they had to do now that their wives had passed away. Linda shared her experience with the Internet:

> I read an article in the Sunday paper, and it discussed a Web site called Widow Net. I went to the site and started reading. This site even had a special posting board dedicated to gays and lesbians, so my hopes were raised. This was only to be a temporary feeling as I soon discovered that activity on the board was

minimal and it was mostly men. Besides, every time I posted on the board, I felt ignored. So I drifted away from it.

On AOL, I found a board where several lesbians had posted about their partners' deaths. I took the plunge and sent a few of them an e-mail, just to let them know they were not alone. I maintained contact with several of them over the course of a few months. One person, especially, was drowning faster than I was, and I found it hard to chat with her, since it continually brought me down even farther.

In contrast to my and Linda's disappointing experiences with online support, Anita and Ellen actually met new partners on the Internet.

THERAPY

Nine lesbian widows noted that they spent time in therapy after their partner's death in order to deal with the tremendous pain they experienced. Six of those nine considered their therapist helpful. Pat, for example, shared how positive this experience was for her:

> For a little over a year I continued having weekly sessions with my therapist. I had determined early on that I would not try to make any major changes in my life during that first year after Betty's death. I thought that it was best to use that time to fully experience the grief I felt and to do the work necessary to move through it without adding more stress to my life. I understand that I was in a fortunate position to be able to do that, and I am grateful for that. Throughout that year I did the hard work necessary to move through the grief, to honor Betty and our love and life together.

On the other hand, Linda found her therapist less than helpful.

> There was no one in my life, friends, family, or others, who knew what it felt like to lose a partner. Sure, many had lost friends or parents, but none had ever lost partners. This made it very difficult to share my grief with them. My grief was so overwhelming to me, I never felt like I could adequately share with anyone the extent of how my entire life had been affected.

> Even the therapist that I was seeing at the time did not get it. Other than losing her parents, she had never felt the loss that I was feeling at this time. My therapist tried to get me to join a support group, but with my work travel schedule, this was not realistic.

Although her therapist may have had the skills to help her, Linda felt that someone who had never been widowed herself could not really understand her level of pain. Linda was able to keep working despite how much she suffered after Tonya's death, but Pam was incapacitated after Sandy passed away.

> I did not work for almost two years. I could barely get out of bed to walk and feed the dog. I was numb. I just did not feel anything. I was on antidepressants (Zoloft) and seeing Andrea, my therapist, twice a week. I could hardly interact with other people.
>
> Some friends were incredible. They called, visited, and took me out to dinner and the movies. We spent time at their house. They even let me stay with them for six weeks when I was in a psychiatric day treatment program. Day treatment was completely worthless, except that I had to get up and go every day. Mostly what I did was sleep and watch TV. Another friend told me that I could call her even at 3:00 a.m. I never did, but I was grateful for that offer.

For almost two years, Pam barely functioned, she was so devastated from losing Sandy. She benefited from spending time with her therapist but not from a hospital day program. Anita found that antidepressants were more helpful to her than talk therapy.

> I went to a therapist. That did not help but I went to see my primary doc and she gave me an antidepressant and that got me through. Plus my friends and being in my home and seeing the things that Holly gave me here.

Many widows found that therapy helped them work through their grief, while a few found it unhelpful. But therapy, friends, and family were only some of the ways we found support.

OTHER SOURCES OF COMFORT

In the midst of our grief, we found comfort in many different ways. Pets and trips were some of the other resources we tapped. Cassie, Pam, and Vera wrote about how comforting their pets were. Cassie explained,

> One of the wonderful blessings that came into my life three years ago that has helped my healing path is Chloe, the most perfect specimen of a canine, a Jack Russell–beagle mix. When I saw Chloe, I saw Fran's soul in her eyes, so I rescued her, and she rescued me. Chloe is now my licensed service dog and we go everywhere together.

Likewise, Vera found that having a pet made a difference in her life.

> After about a month, I suddenly thought, *I want to get a pet.* I ended up getting this wonderful little dog, and she has just made all the difference in the world. I cannot really imagine being without a dog again. She is this funny little dog, and she makes me smile, and she is just wonderful. I had the flu during the semester and, even though she could not go make me a cup of tea, there was another body there and it really did make all the difference.

Pam shared how Sandy's dog, Boo, was a comfort to her after Sandy's death and how sad it was when Boo died.

> About eighteen months after Sandy died, my beloved dog Boo became too ill to continue on. She was a trouper. Some days, she never left my side. But finally it was too much for her and I had her put to sleep. I had her cremated and eventually sprinkled her ashes on Sandy's grave, so they could be together. Perhaps a bit much, but it made me feel better.

Other widows planned and went on trips as part of their recovery process. Janet, for example, made friends on gay trips as well as by inviting people to her home to socialize.

I have monthly potlucks at my house; just safe socializing and introducing new people to other new people. I did some of the planned "Gay Trips" and found a new way of networking. I found more associates, some of whom would become friends, and people to do things with. I was really very careful to watch who I wanted to spend quality time with.

Jane had a peak experience at the Grand Canyon.

In late August and early September of 2001, I made an important trip. I had decided in a "flashbulb moment" the fall before that I should spend what would have been our twenty-fifth anniversary at the Grand Canyon. It was a place Lynn and I had always wanted to go together. I visited a friend in Tucson, another person who kept up with me quite regularly and was a good listener as well as talker, and then drove through the New Age town of Sedona. I was with a best friend from college who was also a lesbian.

I made arrangements to see a spiritualist on my anniversary. She had asked me to bring some questions to ask her, and although I did not advance her any information about why I was there, it did not take her long to discover my distress.

Whether she told me true things she "heard" Lynn say (and one phrase in particular was extremely exact in its tone and language use), or simply was intuitive enough to say things I needed to hear, I cannot discern. All I know is that it was the most healing hour and one-half that I spent in my life. It was almost giving me permission to move on, to say I could continue to love Lynn, yet accept someone else fully into my life. I truly needed to find some joy and some future again, and I needed some kind of reassurance that it would be acceptable.

The trip continued on to the canyon, where we had a great time, so beautiful and so amazing. I felt as though Lynn was there with me, yet I felt calm and quiet alone.

Marilyn traveled with her three adult sons. "The boys and I did some traveling to the Caribbean, something new as we had always been camper travelers. I learned to drive, and the freedom brought much relief from my grief." Lois traveled quite extensively after Joan's death.

I planned trips and went on them, visiting beaches as Joan and I had talked about doing many times. I went to Mexico, Florida, and Costa Rica. It was a way of being able to get some literal distance on the experience, to sort of jolt myself into still being alive. I took my daughter and granddaughter to Disney World, a new experience for all of us, and to the beach, the first time for them.

Joy related how difficult it was for her to travel to Provincetown again after Barbara's death.

I would go to P'town every summer and rent a boathouse apartment on the water, just a couple of blocks down the street from the P'town Inn, and invite acquaintances to come stay over. I never did much with them. I only wanted to stay in the boathouse and read my book on the sun deck while they went off every day to explore things to do. They thought me weird, although a few of them came to know that I was still grieving over Barbara, but they loved staying in my apartment and I liked having them there. Somehow hearing them laughing in the night soothed my effort to sleep in peace.

Shirley took a vacation to Florida about six months after Terry's death. Ellen returned to Hawaii, where Kate had died, around the time of the first anniversary of her death. Irene did not specify where she went, but she wrote, "One of the things I did was go away by myself, soon after MJ's death, to have time away and time to myself outside of where everything happened."

Some widows found comfort in visiting places where they had been with their lovers, but Irene found that unhelpful. She also mentioned some other things that did not help her. "Things that did not help were going to the cemetery, spending time at places where we had done things together, and, most of all, expecting myself to feel better and accomplish changes in my life before I was ready."

Just as Donna wrote that music had helped ease her pain as Randi was dying, she discovered that another musical experience was healing after Randi's death.

In the depths of grief, which seemed unending, I made myself a promise: "If I see anything that makes my heart sing, I will do it." A year after Randi's death, a friend gave me a ticket to a steel band concert. Entranced, I hung over the balcony railing and poked my friends, telling them in a whisper, "I have to do that." After the performance I asked the director if I could take lessons, and he told me I could come to the next rehearsal, since I could read music and play at least one other instrument. Such happy music! I could hardly wait. Over the summer I learned the rhythms, the harmonies, the tunes, all of which were foreign to me.

Rose and Cassie found that having items that belonged to their partners provided them with some level of comfort. Rose explained,

> I have lots of "things" that were Steph's (e.g., books, paintings, gardening stuff, kitchen stuff, some clothing, etc.). And of course, I still have things that we got together or gifts that she gave me. I did not spend much time in the "leave everything the way it was when she died" stage, but, on the other hand, I have only disposed of a little bit of it.
>
> When she moved out, she left me what she/we thought I would use or like, so it is still part of my life. The only part where I am really stuck is her writings. I have all the cards, notes, and letters she wrote to me, from the beginning of our relationship. I do not want to get rid of them, but I also still cannot bear to read them. They are by far my most intimate reminders of who she was, how she loved me, and how our life together was. For now they sit in files and piles in my study.

Cassie shared what she missed about Fran and the comfort she took in Fran's picture:

> She enriched those nine months of my life with her humor, her tenderness, and her touch, and her singing love songs in my ear while we danced. I miss her cooking, her subtle sexual cartoon drawings that she hid for me to find and tease me with. I loved her curiosity, her serenity, and her delight in playing with children and feeding the little birds and the nicknames she gave everyone she loved. Most of all I miss her integrity and reverence for life. She truly loved life and people, and I do believe that Fran had completed her circle of life when she died. I keep her

picture on my dresser, I talk with her often, and I know she lives
within me.

In contrast to Cassie and Rose, Vera immediately began removing
some of Nancy's things from their home.

> My style is to do stuff right away. So, even on the Monday
> right after Nancy died, one of my friends drove me home and
> stayed with me for a while before some other friends came over.
> The first thing I did was to take all of Nancy's pills and flush
> them down the toilet. And then after the next two weeks, I
> started going through a lot of her stuff and I moved some things
> right away. It felt really important to me to try and make the
> space my own in some ways.
> Everything about this house is filled with Nancy's pres-
> ence—from a framed photograph that she took, to gifts that
> were to both of us. So, it was not wiping Nancy out, it was just
> making the space mine. I needed to do that, so I did that, I did
> quite a bit of that. I got rid of a bookcase, got rid of an old stereo,
> got some plants, just sort of did enough rearranging that it felt as
> if I were making it more mine.

Irene explained what she did with some of MJ's belongings. "I
took MJ's things that I could not let go of and put them together in a
box, a tribute box, where they still remain. I looked at it many times in
the first year, and now I have not opened it in over a year."

Others noted how difficult it was to move out of the house they had
shared with their lover. Maureen, for example, talked about selling
their home. "It was terrible to sell Robin's and my house, but the
hardest part was actually leaving. There were so many dreams there
for us and so many parts of her I did not want to leave." Moving was
difficult for Heather too.

> One unexpected hard part was the first time I moved after she
> died. How could I move without giving her my new address and
> phone number? How could I not try to freeze my life so that I
> could still imagine her in it?

In the midst of our grief, we each found different sources of support and comfort. The majority of us had the support of friends, but

not all. Some had a supportive family but many did not. Some found Internet resources that helped, but others did not. Some took trips while others found solace at home.

Married women whose husbands die are recognized by others as widows and receive the support of family and friends. The married widow may even receive cards and words of comfort from colleagues, acquaintances, and neighbors. This is not necessarily true for lesbians. The majority of the widows in this book received support primarily from their lesbian family rather than their family of origin. Actually, the majority did not expect to receive support outside of their local lesbian community, although some were surprised when they did. As with the lesbian widows who were hurt by fellow lesbians at funerals or memorial services (Chapter 7), so too those lesbians who hurt the most in the months after the death of their life partner were those hurt by fellow lesbians from whom they had expected to receive support and did not.

Chapter 10

Complications

Lesbian widows in this book faced three major complications that married widows do not. One was discrimination in legal and financial matters because our relationships are not legal marriages. The second complication was the lack of support groups for lesbian widows, and the third was the lack of written materials specifically for lesbians. These difficulties contributed to our sense of being invisible.

LEGAL DISCRIMINATION

Seven of the twenty-four lesbian widows, almost one-third, told me that they had encountered hassles over legal and financial affairs that, if they had been married, they would not have faced. I thought that Marilyn spoke quite clearly about this dilemma:

> I am a widow. The law does not say so. My tax form does not say so. Neither do any of the countless forms that I fill out that include marital status say so. But every time I check off the box that says single, I want to scream and white it out and write "widow." But I am a lesbian who has lost her female partner, so in most places I am not accorded the status of widow. When it came time to settle Cheryl's estate, I was a class D beneficiary—no relationship whatsoever, a roommate, a friend, the lady next door.
>
> It does not seem to matter that we lived in a monogamous, loving relationship for thirty-one years, or that we coparented three wonderful children. It does not seem to matter that those children have severe developmental disabilities and, although they are now legally adults, I continue to be a single parent. What am I thinking? We were each always single parents!!! Our home, our cars, our belongings—the law said that they legally are hers and mine so I will

pay taxes on half of all we owned and all of some that we had purchased together but were registered in her name. After all I am not a
legal widow any more than I was a legal wife or a legal coparent.

Not a legal wife, not a legal coparent, not a legal widow. Marilyn
was invisible from a legal point of view. And because she was not legally related to Cheryl, she had to struggle with legal challenges that
would not be part of a married widow's grief journey. In Vera's case,
it was Nancy's pension that was denied to her because their relationship was not recognized as a legitimate marriage.

I was the beneficiary of Nancy's life insurance, but I lost twenty-
two years of her pension because I was not a legal spouse. She
could not even have designated it to me as a beneficiary. Only if
I had been a legal spouse could I have gotten it. That is a lot of
money, but it is not that I want the money. It is the principle of it.

Others shared their negative experiences with the legal system in
trying to settle their lover's estate. Beverly thought that they had
taken care of everything by putting their estates in a trust, but she
found out differently.

One thing that I was surprised about, as I reflect back, was that
we never were that interested in pursuing trying to get it legal for
gay people to be able to get married. We would like that, but we
never worked hard on it with those people who are working at it.
We had everything in a trust so that whichever one of us survived would be able to continue living as we had been, and then
after we were both gone, the estate, or whatever was left, would
be divided up, half going to her son, or other family members if
he was no longer here, and my half to my family.
But, even with everything in trust, I was really upset that, at a
time when I did not feel like doing it, I had to do an inventory of
all the things that were in the trust. Things like that, had we been
married, I would not have had to do.

Irene wrote that legal hassles nearly drove her to suicide:

Frantic discussions with the lawyer about my limited rights in
settling her estate drove me to the brink of despair. I wanted it all

to end. I contemplated suicide. I planned how I could do it. I only refrained because I could not do that to my parents.

Cassie expressed her anger in dealing with estate issues: "Being a lesbian definitely affected what was happening to me. I struggled to accept, with anger, my limited rights under state and federal law to what she had left me of her estate." Ellen protested the unfairness of legal issues she had to deal with:

> I went through so many ridiculous things with the legal system. If a person leaves their money to someone who is not the legal spouse, you have to track down all the relatives or prove they are dead. A good reason for having same-sex marriage.

Without legal recognition of our relationships, without the right to marry, lesbian widows will continue to encounter a legal system that does not recognize them as legitimate spouses. As a result of not being able to be legally married, Vera lost Nancy's pension, and Marilyn, Beverly, Cassie, and Ellen faced difficulties in settling their partner's estate, all situations that a married woman would never have to deal with, and all at a time when they were emotionally already struggling. Traci faced the additional stress of threats from Dana's ex-husband.

> Dana's ex-husband demanded money from Dana's investments for his three children. I agreed to this settlement because I did not want to go through a lengthy and expensive court battle. He threatened me with exposing my lifestyle, and I could not afford to be out of work.

Because our relationships are invisible and unrecognized as far as the law is concerned, legal discrimination is just one more factor that complicates our grief. No matter how many years we were together in a loving relationship, no matter how much care and devotion we showed to our partner as she was dying, our relationships do not exist (legally). They are invisible. If we had the right to marry, we would be allowed to collect our partner's pension and Social Security benefits without question, take family leave when our partner was ill, and be automatically recognized as the benefactor of our partner's estate.

SUPPORT GROUPS

The second area where lesbians face complications that are usually not encountered by married women is the lack of support groups. After my mother passed away, two months after Emily died, I felt like I needed more help than my friends could give me, but I did not know where to turn. I felt stuck in grief. The therapist I met with during the ten months that Emily was dying helped me tremendously, especially in working through some of the negative aspects of the relationship that bothered me. But I felt like my grief after Em's death and my mother's was a natural response to my situation, and I should not have to pay a therapist to listen to me talk about and cry for them.

Upon the urging of a friend, I contacted hospice, not sure that they would be willing or able to provide services to a lesbian. Since I was in a new community, however, I felt free to be out without worrying about outing Em. I knew there was no point in asking for help if I could not tell the whole story. Through hospice I was able to attend a six-week general grief group. I had been assured that the group facilitator would keep the conversation on grief and not allow my sexual orientation to be an issue. The five group members had different kinds of loss. One had lost an adult child, one her husband, one her sister, and one her mother; I was the only lesbian widow. But we bonded over our common grief. It was helpful to hear others' stories and share my own.

The second and most helpful service for me from hospice was a volunteer to meet with me. Sue listened to me tell my story and cry week after week. I found it hard to believe someone who did not know me would be willing to donate her time to do that, and I was amazed at her ability to listen to me tell many of the same things over and over yet be nothing but supportive.

Dale and Jane were both fortunate to find grief support groups specifically for lesbians. Dale wrote,

> I had a good therapist who also knew Carol. I still felt very alone and it has been an incredible journey. I eventually found a lesbian bereavement group that was incredibly helpful. It was so helpful being with other lesbians who were in different stages of grieving but also suffering the same kind of grief.

Jane had to make a lot of phone calls before she finally found a lesbian group.

I decided to seek some professional help. I thought a group would help, but finding one would prove to be very difficult. I made at least two dozen calls, one person leading me to another. I tried several places. They had grief groups of mixed gender and/or women only, but definitely not lesbian oriented. Somehow, women discussing the loss of their father, son, or friend did not really relate to me. I understood they could have the same sense of loss, but there was no commiseration about my situation, no understanding.

Surprisingly, in a big city, I found lesbian groups sadly omitted from many grief support programs. I tried the various cancer groups, even those dedicated to women, but to no avail. The least helpful place (and subsequently most disappointing) was the Gay and Lesbian Center. The bereavement program is sadly lacking in follow-up organization, and I felt like a nonentity there. The counselors were too young and inexperienced as psychologists to understand what I was going through.

Finally I was led to someone at the Visiting Nurse Service's grief support program. Normally, the services they provide are directed at those who have been involved in their Home Hospice care program, but I was interviewed by the director of the grief support groups, by happenstance a lesbian, and one with a particular interest in forming lesbian-only and mixed-gender gay groups. I found her one-on-one counseling very helpful. Although I could not keep that up on a regular basis, she saw me several times, and then asked me to join a lesbian group she had just started. The group was very small, just three of us in total, lasting about eight weeks. It was most helpful for understanding the grief process, what to look for, what to expect, what was "normal."

I joined another group after that, also led by the same facilitator. I found this group to also be helpful in the sense that it provided a feelings outlet for me, but as far as progress or discovery, not as helpful as the first go-round. The most important thing was to realize that one is not totally alone in the process. No matter how differently one experiences a loss, the commonality is that you are going through the process of living without the loved one. It was *most* helpful to speak with other lesbians about the loss of their partner. Whether it had been a long or short-term relationship did not make a difference.

Jane's last point, that the length of the relationship did not make a difference, was what I also found to be true for the twenty-four widows in this book. Whether the relationship had lasted five months or thirty-seven years, the loss was traumatic. Vera actually found more than one support group, but she still felt that she was not helped much by any of them.

My sister, who was widowed, was a huge advocate of grief groups. So I looked into what was available around here and there were two hospice organizations. One of them runs a variety of grief groups, and they happened to be starting a group, just three weeks after Nancy's death. It was a closed group, time-limited, and each week was going to deal with a different aspect of grief.

It was not a good experience. Not a good experience at all. The person who ran it was not very good. She had a mannerism that did not seem sincere, and she did not really have any personal experience with grief. They ended up getting a second person who was better to do it along with her, but I did not like her very well. The people who did end up being in the group (twelve to fourteen) were mostly women, but I was the only person who identified myself as a lesbian. I say that because my friend, who was there and who also was a lesbian, did not ever identify herself as one.

There were several people in the group who were clearly conservative Christians, and god only knows what they thought of the fact that I was a lesbian. No one ever said anything to me, but it did not feel terribly comfortable to me. And on the third week we were supposed to bring in pictures of the person who had died, and everybody brought some. People "oohed and ahhed" over the pictures, but mine zoomed around the circle and came back to me. I thought I might not want to go because I was avoiding my grief, but that did not feel right. I just stopped going. It did not feel like a life-enhancing experience at all.

The other option that I had was another hospice group that only runs a support group once a month for women. I went two or three times. The person who ran it was a self-identified born-again Christian, but, interestingly, the first time I went, it was just me and her and she was okay. The other times I went there were only one or two other people. It was not bad, but it just did not feel like much of a life-enhancing experience for me, and it was really disappointing. I felt like I was failing my sister, but it just did not work for me.

I am a big believer in therapy, and my therapist had moved away. After about a year's worth of not successful searching, I ended up about a year ago with a really wonderful therapist, and she said it was really okay to not be going to a group since I had a really good support system.

Samantha, fortunately, did not have the long and difficult search that Vera did. She attended a one-day bereavement workshop that she found useful and informative.

I did a bereavement workshop after the first-year anniversary of Marie's death. I think that was very helpful. I had to wait a year for it to come around because they did not have enough people to fill the group out the first year. It was geared toward gay people that had lost a loved one. I think that I was able to get out a lot of the hurt and pain that I had been feeling, but even so it has been a long hard process.

Four more women reported that they looked for grief support groups but did not find them, not even in agencies that provided other services to lesbians. Janet, for example, shared her frustration:

I checked the hospitals for bereavement groups, but did not qualify, as I was not a relation of Chris, just a "friend." I checked the Lambda Center and nothing was offered. I checked with cancer groups and was not refused but was not really welcome to join because her death was different (a police officer shot in the line of duty). I checked with the widows' service through the Highway Patrol and got very little acknowledgment as it was not a "real" marriage. My heartache was no different from that of a man-woman relationship but no one wanted to recognize it as such.

Maureen was angry that no lesbian support groups were offered by her local lesbian cancer center.

> I think being a lesbian made a difference in my grieving process because it was not so easy to pick up a support group. There are not really any lesbian support groups for widows. There are a lot of breakup and recovery groups, but I did not stop loving her and did not feel like I need the same kind of support they offer in those groups.
>
> I was surprised at how out of touch the lesbian community on the whole is. When Robin was sick, we contacted the local lesbian cancer project and found that there were not any support groups. I find it very hard to participate in the big fund-raiser for the group every year because there was *no* support.

Jane noted that there are AIDS groups for gay men, and support groups for cancer victims, but no groups for surviving lesbian widows:

> The grief process is an individual and private one, yet I do not think it can be tolerated alone. I have seen other gay or lesbian "halves" who still struggle with their loss, yet they do not seem to actively participate in getting themselves out of the rut they find themselves in. I think it is so important for there to be some outlet for people to talk, to share. The lack of grief groups unrelated to AIDS for men or cancer support groups that cater to just women is rare, almost nonexistent from my point of view.

Samantha shared that her personal struggle to find support is what motivated her to share her story in this book so that others would not face that same struggle:

> It has been a difficult road for me simply because I did not know where to turn for support. The traditional arenas seemed to be full of older people that I could not relate to in my circumstances, even though I was eight years older than Marie. Where I live, it seems that the gist of cancer victims, survivors, whatever, are older, more traditional types that I felt no alliance with, i.e., heterosexuals who had lived full lives.

I so lost track of myself during the course of her cancer that I found that I had no personal support once the dust had cleared and I found myself alone. If I can help anyone at all through their pain, then I want to make this count for something.

Vera recounted her attempts to create a support group for herself after she found other bereavement groups unhelpful:

I tried to create support for myself where I could. There were two women who had each lost a previous partner, and they both said they would come and talk to me. A couple months after Nancy died, I had them down for lunch and they talked about their experiences. That was interesting, but they are not women that I would normally hang around with. It was interesting to hear their experiences, but it did not really do a lot for me.

My friend Margaret's next-door neighbor lost her husband three years ago, so I had breakfast with her one time and we talked about it. I tried to connect with other women who had lost a partner in various ways, but I did not feel that I had a real support system.

Only two out of the twenty-four widows in this book found bereavement support groups specifically for lesbians in which to participate. Four more actively looked for groups and could not find them. Vera expressed her frustration in finding support this way:

If I could have waved a magic wand as a lesbian, I would have created a support system for myself. One that was already in place. An ongoing support group for lesbians who have gone through loss. Because I do think that our experiences are different as lesbians just because, even though everyone has been very supportive all through the process, the fact is that I did not get the type of public recognition that I otherwise might have. It just feels different somehow.

Although I found some comfort in attending a general grief group, I think it was my own desperation to get help, rather than the group itself, that was the real reason I benefited from it. I know I would have profited more if a lesbian-only group had been available. Although I had supportive lesbian friends, none of them had experienced the death of a partner. As other widows have already commented, if you have not been widowed yourself, you just cannot imagine how painful it is. The majority of the widows who contacted me commented on how good it felt to them to talk to me, knowing that I had experienced the loss of a partner too.

WRITTEN MATERIALS

In our search for support, we discovered that not only were there no support groups for us, there were also no grief books written specifically for lesbian widows. In the absence of such a book, several women shared what books they read that gave them some level of comfort. Donna, for example, told me that she had found *A Woman's Book of Grieving* by Nessa Rapoport helpful. Beverly shared two books in which she found some consolation:

> As time went on, two books were helpful. One was *Cancer in Two Voices* by Sandra Butler and Barbara Rosenblum. Even though their book was mostly about the illness and their experience was somewhat different from Virginia's and mine, there were many similarities. Since this was close to the period I had been experiencing some of the same things, it seemed like I was really sharing with somebody what it felt like to go through that.
>
> I also found the book *Healing After Loss*. I'm not very religious, and these are daily meditations for working through grief, not all of which are religious. A lot of the things that are said in this book felt so right to me or were exactly what I was experiencing.

Linda was disappointed in the lack of written material for lesbians.

> I had hoped that by reading books, I would understand how to get some support during this journey. Reading books had become one of the most effective methods I have utilized to understand issues in my life and take corrective action. However, this was not to be, as there were really no books written for lesbians who had lost partners.
>
> A few months ago I read the book written by Chastity Bono about losing her partner, and I identified more with that book than anything else I had read. I wanted to write a letter to Ms.

Bono to say thank you. However, I never felt like I could get the letter to correctly convey those feelings. Besides, she probably would never see it anyway.

Nora was helped by one book in particular.

The most useful book I was given was Rabbi Kushner's *Why Bad Things Happen to Good People.* His philosophy is that God does not send these awful things to punish you, test you, or make you a stronger person. They just happen. Also, God cannot reverse the irreversible. But God does send you help and you get the help you *need,* not necessarily what you *want.* Important distinction there.

Jane identified several books she found helpful:

Several of the books that were helpful I mention here: *Living with Loss* by Ellen Sue Stern (Dell Paperback; written for the heterosexual, but easy to change the pronouns for oneself), *Living with Grief* edited by Joyce D. Davidson and Kenneth J. Doka (Hospice Foundation of America—I liked understanding what the professionals look for in patients/clients), and *A Grief Observed* by C. S. Lewis (Bantam Books). I would not say it was the faith parts of any of these books that attracted me but the relationship I could manufacture in my head with the author(s), understanding their feelings while feeling as though they understood mine.

Vera was ambivalent about books she read.

Books were sort of helpful. The hospice group used a book called *Understanding Grief,* which I read. Some stuff I knew, some I did not, so that was interesting. Another friend recommended a book I really liked called *Seven Choices* by Elizabeth Neelz. She herself was widowed young but there is stuff that people can apply to other difficult times in their lives. Several other people gave me other books and meditations about grieving and I liked those. One or two I kept by my bed and would close my eyes and just open a page and read one every day for a while and that was good. I ordered a book from *Lesbian Con-*

nection and I think the title was *Write from the Heart: Lesbians Healing from Heartache.* It was both for breakups and those who lost partners to death. It was okay, but it did not do very much for me. It was better than nothing.

I think Vera's sentiment "It was better than nothing" pretty well sums up how most of us felt about any books we read. No book was available specifically for us, but reading anything close to our experience helped.

DISENFRANCHISED GRIEF

Professionals use the term *disenfranchised grief* to describe a situation where a partner experiences a loss that is not openly acknowledged (Doka, 2002). Society does not accept our relationships, and our losses are consequently not recognized. We are not legal widows; plus there are very few support groups for us and even fewer written resources. This makes it even more important, however, for lesbian service organizations to sensitize themselves to the needs of widows and begin to provide supportive services for them.

Chapter 11

The First Two Years

Even with all the support I initially received, I noticed that, around three months after Emily's death, friends stopped calling on me as much. I understood. They had their own lives to live. I knew that I had to find my own way through the grief recovery process. Rose and Pam noted this about their friends as well. Rose explained,

> My family was too far away to be much support, although Steph's family did help. At least we could share the grief and the memories. Friends tried to be supportive, and I appreciated their efforts. Those who knew me only casually knew that Steph had been living out of state, so I do not think they could fully comprehend the depth of my sorrow. Closer friends had a better sense of my loss.
>
> I knew from previous experience that friends who have not grieved the loss of a partner just did not understand the amount of time it takes to get on with living. After a few weeks or months, most expect you to be "back to normal." No matter how compassionate they want to be, they cannot relate to an ongoing grief process. So any grief work after two or three months is done alone.

Pam knew her friends did the best they could. Plus, she admitted that she held back from asking for more help.

> Eventually people started to drift away and get back to their lives. It seemed everyone I knew was part of a couple and suddenly I was not. When the phone stopped ringing on a regular basis, I was adrift. I was afraid of being too needy and was very guarded with my feelings. I did not reach out very often or very well. Those first holidays and birthdays were incredibly hard for me.

No matter how much support she receives initially, in the end a widow must still deal with her grief alone. She is the one left with lonely nights, the one who does not have someone to come home to, the one who must build a future without a partner. In the last few chapters, I have shared our experiences immediately after our partner's death, where and how we found support, and the complications faced by lesbian but not married widows. In this chapter, I give an overview of what the first two years of being widowed were like for us.

THE FIRST YEAR

Throughout the first year of grieving, there were many anniversary reactions to face. Anniversary reactions are unsolicited emotional responses to days or events that remind us of our deceased partner (Rando, 1988). Lois's experience with anniversary reactions was common.

> That whole first year was punctuated by reliving the anniversaries. I think that the emotional level of the trauma I went through during those seventeen months of Joan's illness was largely unexperienced emotionally until the year after she died. I remembered every day we went to the oncologist, every time we went to the hospital, every bit of bad news, every sweet moment. I would cry and scream and just lay in bed and shake. Or find someone to talk to and just talk and talk.

Lois related two common experiences. In the first year, every day that was special when our partner was alive we now experienced alone. For those of us who were our partner's caretaker for a period of time before she died, we could no longer put our grief on hold. The full force of what happened finally hit us. Janet related how difficult holidays were for her:

> The first year after, I hated holidays with passion. I did not go home and I did not celebrate them. I would send cards and gifts to my nieces and nephews. Valentine's Day was a cruel joke, nothing more. I kept thinking that, although I moved on with life, I never closed the chapter of my life with Chris. I never did say good-bye. I became aware of the phrase "It's better to have

loved and lost than never to have loved." I knew it fit me, and I would not love that hard or well again.

For me, Emily's birthday was an especially difficult day. I talked to her mother and sister, who lived out of state, and offered to take flowers to Em's grave for them. On her birthday, I sat at the cemetery, talked to her, and cried. For her mother, I took a pot of mums; for her sister, a teacup with yellow roses in it (tea and teacups had special significance in their family); and I laid a single yellow rose on her grave from me. Afterward I joined a couple of friends who had been members of Em's support team for dinner, and we talked about how it was hard to believe that nearly a whole year had gone by.

Heather, a psychologist doing clinical work, found herself experiencing grief at an emotional level that defied any clinical knowledge she had.

The first year I was surprised to have anniversary reactions. I had heard of them, of course, but somehow thought I was immune. I found myself experiencing them even though I was not consciously aware of the date.

Similar to Heather, I have found it true that I always feel it in my body when it is the anniversary of Em's or my mother's death, whether or not I am conscious of the date. As I approached the one-year mark after Emily's death, I had the professional knowledge to know that it might be a difficult time for me. However, around the same time I started to have a desire to stop being so much of a hermit. I wanted to make some new friends, friends who would know me as a person, rather than as part of a couple. I really felt guilty, though, for feeling that way. In my journal, I quoted a section from the book *A Time to Grieve* which said that finding pleasure in life did not mean I was being disloyal to Emily or that I no longer cared, that it was okay to laugh again. So I pushed myself, made myself go to some lesbian social groups, and ended up making some wonderful friends.

And then September 11 happened. Like most of America, I was glued to the television set. Suddenly the whole nation was mourning.

Every time I listen to the news or watch TV I find myself going into that kind of shell-shocked condition I had the night that Em was diagnosed with cancer. I just have to shut off the TV; it is too much to bear. I cannot handle this on top of my own grief. I am so grateful Em and I had ten months to say good-bye to each other and that I have mementos and scrapbooks to read and remember. Unlike the families and friends of those who died in the terrorist attack on Sept. 11.

Ellen had a similar reaction to 9/11.

> I was in Hawaii when Sept. 11 happened and had to stay an extra week. I had gone on a personal pilgrimage, and now it was this huge collective level of trauma and loss. This makes you view life differently. For me, it was like taking my insides and putting them outside. The whole country was grieving.

The anniversary of Em's death was one month after 9/11 happened. I was depressed that whole month; it felt like I could feel the grief of the country on top of my own grief. For me, anniversary reactions throughout that first year had been like small ocean waves, and then the first anniversary of Emily's death was more like a huge wave that knocked my feet out from under me.

I spent a lot of time thinking about what to do to commemorate the anniversary of her death. At one point, I thought about asking friends to join me for a commemorative service, but somehow that did not feel right. In the end, I did several things. I remembered how Emily had me send thank-you notes and roses to the women who had been part of her support team as she was dying, and I decided to send notes to these women, thanking them for all they had done to support both of us the previous year. Another thing I did was reflect on where I was emotionally the year before compared to now, one year later.

A year ago, my heart felt like it had been ripped open, jagged edges, raw pain. Today it feels like the jagged edges are smoother, the wound is beginning to close yet is still very tender. I can imagine healing light on my heart, like salve on a sore wound.

On the actual anniversary of Em's death, I decided to attend a professional conference to try to not think about it. Mistake! I left the conference after a few hours with a splitting headache and went home to cry. I then created an anniversary ritual based on ideas described in a hospice newsletter I had received. I lit one candle to represent my grief and to remind myself that the depth of my pain reflected the depth of our love. I lit a second candle for my courage—the courage to confront my sorrow and go on living. A third candle was for my memories—the times we laughed, cried, were angry, silly, all the love and caring. And a fourth candle was to cherish the special place in my heart for Emily.

A few weeks later, on the anniversary of the private memorial service I had arranged the previous year, I had the opportunity to meet with my minister to talk about Emily. As much as I appreciated the time my hospice volunteer had given me in the previous year, I felt like I needed to talk some things out with someone who had actually known Emily. Afterward, I wrote in my journal,

I have been in a winter time in my soul for the last year. Even when the seasons of the earth changed to spring and summer, I was locked into winter inside. Now outside the leaves are starting to turn colors and the beauty of fall is here, but inside I feel like I am starting to see the first signs of spring. Like it is still cold inside, but it is as if I see birds in trees and bushes. Glimmers of hope, a sense that things are about to thaw. I need to turn my focus now to my own healing instead of reliving the time of Emily's illness and death.

It occurred to me, then, that the anniversary of Em's death was also the one-year anniversary of my facing life alone. This time I lit a candle for that new life. It felt like I had given myself permission in the previous year to grieve, and now I was giving myself permission to go on..

One last thing I did around that time was to write Em a letter. I told her how I missed her and how hard the last year had been. But I also told her that I could tell that things were changing for me, from focusing on her death to starting to think about how to create a new life for myself.

I know that you would not approve of my new life. You would not approve of my involvement in the lesbian social groups I have joined. You would not approve of my coming out at work, to students and faculty and administration alike. You would not approve of the ad I put in *Lesbian Connection*, asking for volunteers for my lesbian widow research project, or of my plans to write a book about the subject. But I like my new life. I like living openly and honestly.

Seven is a number of completion, and we were together, as lovers, for seven years. Our time together is completed. Thank you for loving me, for giving me those years of your life. My life is so much richer for having known and loved you.

What I was doing was trying to find meaning in my loss. I needed to have an explanation for what had happened that would help me find some closure and not leave me feeling angry, hurt, bitter, or stuck in the past.

Ellen shared the creative way she honored the first anniversary of Kate's death. She, too, was coming to terms with what had happened to her.

> At the first-year memorial, all I wanted to do was be at the cemetery and be quiet. Friends were afraid of my grief, afraid I would go too far. I spent six hours at the cemetery in a deep mournful state. My sisters and friends were around for the memorial two days later. We went to Mass. I made displays of pictures of Kate's life. I had sushi because that was Kate's favorite food. Someone brought helium-filled balloons; we let our balloons go with a prayer. A hawk started circling the balloons as they rose. I felt like the year had come to closure. I had done everything I needed to do. I had felt the depth of pain but also gratitude.

For Ellen, the one-year anniversary brought a sense of closure. Lois shared how she commemorated the first anniversary of Joan's death: "We had another retreat a year later, and several of the care team went with me to Colorado to release Joan's ashes. Now we have made a ritual of getting together for Joan's birthday."

Rather than describing what they did on the first anniversary of their partner's death, other widows commented on how emotionally difficult it was. Rose wrote that she had not been able to cry for the whole first year after Steph died because she just felt numb. But on the first anniversary of Steph's death, the tears flowed.

> One year, of course, was difficult. Not only did I react to the fact of the first anniversary of Steph's death, but the fact that she died on Christmas Day complicates the entire holiday season. As much as I loved it before, I just cannot get into the spirit of celebrating any more.
>
> A few friends and I joke about her timing: Steph always did go for the dramatic! Just to make sure we never forget her, she picked the biggest holiday of the year to die. I miss the celebrating in some ways, but it just does not feel like it fits anymore. I am most likely to spend the day quietly by myself, calling my siblings during the day but otherwise not doing "Christmas things." It's not that I spend the day depressed, but rather that I

use it for quiet reflection. Maybe that will change someday, but for now it seems to fit.

Irene wrote about how painful the first anniversary was for her, noting that the shock that had sheltered her from the full impact of MJ's death in the beginning was no longer there: "At the first anniversary, and first holidays, I ached for MJ. It was like reliving the deepest grief only without the numbness of the initial shock, making it worse." Irene aptly described the healing process, a process that is cyclical, not linear.

At the first-year anniversary, Samantha seemed to be feeling guilty that she had lived and Marie had died. But this is another common reaction to loss: survivor guilt.

> At the first anniversary, I reflected on how Marie was eight years younger than I was, so her cancer and the aggressiveness of her illness caught me by surprise. It was exactly one year and three months from the time she was diagnosed to the time that she died. I thought it should have been me. I had not, after all, just figured out what I wanted to do with my life the way Marie had, and I was not the human dynamo that she was. I felt that I was so much more ordinary and therefore expendable.

In contrast to Irene and Samantha, Maureen told me that the first anniversary had not been that bad. What had been difficult for her in that first year was the days that she and Robin had scheduled a trip or a party or some activity. By the first anniversary, the date of every activity that she and Robin had planned was past.

> The one-year anniversary came and went like any other day. I think I was handling it better then, because at this point all of the things we had planned had come and gone. The concerts, vacation time, Easter dinner we planned, the birth of the baby, etc. I just thought it would be easier when I got to things I had planned for myself after Robin was gone.

Even though she wrote that the first anniversary was not upsetting to her, Maureen admitted to me that, after she completed the questionnaire, she realized that she had unfinished business over Robin's death and went back into therapy.

THE SECOND YEAR

As the first year after our partner's death ended and we moved into the second year, the grief was still there, but, in general, the pain was not quite as intense. I still had occasional dreams of Emily and still talked to her, but not as often.

I dreamed about Em last night. I can't remember it clearly except at the end. I was talking to a woman and told her I needed to tell her about Em. Then instead of me just telling her about Em, Emily was there with us, talking with us. Then it was time for Em to go and she started walking up some stairs. I stood at the bottom of the stairs. Em turned to me, and I thanked her for having spent time with us. I felt deeply connected and close to her. When I woke up, I just laid there awhile, feeling close to Em, remembering that soul mate kind of connection we had. And then I started crying, missing her.

A few months later, another journal entry read,

There must be a purpose for my life that does not include Em, and her death set me free to pursue it. Yet I will forever appreciate the gifts she gave me and treasure the memory of our time together.

I was beginning to shift my focus from holding onto my relationship with Em to thinking about what my future held. Jane related her experience in the second year after Lynn's death:

> The second summer without Lynn, about one and one-half years after her death, I was again feeling lost and confused. I started to look for another professional in earnest. I interviewed one woman who wanted to prescribe Prozac, which I was vehemently opposed to because I thought it treated the symptoms, not the problem. I interviewed another therapist, and she felt more comfortable to me, so I saw her.
>
> The idea of needing paid psychiatric help was unappealing, but I felt I had no choice. I knew my friends were becoming more and more tired of my depression and depressive states, and I was also tired of feeling that way and did not know how to get out of it.
>
> I am not sure now what exactly this therapist would say or do to get me to talk about the things bothering me. I think there was always a sense of "What did I accomplish/learn/realize today?" I could also "deprogram" with my roommate—a very wise, un-

derstanding young woman who had helped me in a very passive sense since the previous fall. I found myself thinking about the questions and answers during the week after a counseling session and trying to work things out in my head.

After a year of struggling on her own, Jane sought professional help, which empowered her to not only grieve over the past but also figure out what to do with her life in the future. Nora, dealing with the death of both her son, Max, and her partner, Anne, also sought help, but of a different kind.

During the second year I felt more stable but I was still subject to fits of deep depression when I wanted to give up on life. I wanted to be with Anne and Max. Shortly after the third anniversary of Max's death and the second anniversary of becoming Anne's lover, I went to see a kinesiologist. My goal was to let go of grief. It was the best thing I ever did for myself, more effective than any of the therapy I had done. It made me put a searchlight on why I was holding onto that grief. I had to admit it was my security blanket. I held onto it because it was the only way I knew of proving my love for Anne and Max. I was able to let that go and commit to honoring them with love.

After struggling for more than a year, Nora was finally able to release the pain and come to a place of peace. Her comment that her grief was like a security blanket is a good metaphor for how hard it was for all of us to let go of our pain because it felt like it was the pain that kept us linked to our deceased partner. Rather than holding onto the pain, however, we found that we healed when we were able to hold onto our memories instead.

Pat felt she had done the emotional work she needed to do in the first year after Betty's death but related how she had to deal with legal, financial, and practical details during the second year:

After the first year was over I still had many things to do to finish the paperwork of changing all the things that were held jointly to my name. I had not even tried to take any but the basic required actions until I felt ready to handle it emotionally. I was able, after the year of working through the grief, to once more turn my attention to the mundane.

One is amazed at how many things have to be done and how long it takes to even find all that must be changed at some point. Even now, after two and one-half years, there are still things that need to be finished, i.e., cleaning out closets, disposing of extra cameras, sports equipment, having her name removed from mailing lists, etc. However, now it is just a matter of making or taking the time to do these things rather than being unable to face them.

I think Pat's comment about making the time for it rather than being unable to face doing it is a good example of the transition many of us began making during the second year. The pain was not gone and the grieving was not over, but we were beginning to make peace with what had happened. Ellen described her continued experience of Kate's presence in the second year after Kate's death:

During the second year, I had incredible dreams, continued in therapy, and had a good connection with Kate. I recycled through another level of grief about halfway through the year. I felt like I was back at the beginning again.

This sense of "recycling" that Ellen described is another metaphor about how we experience grief. Grief work is not a straight line. It has ups and downs, backs and forths, twists and turns. Just when we think we are finished grieving, we find ourselves grieving once again.

By the two-year anniversary, the majority of us were realizing that, although the pain was still there, it was less intense. My journal reflected my own ambivalence as that anniversary day drew near. On one hand, it was still painful. On the other hand, I felt like I was doing better.

I am starting to understand that, no matter how busy I am, my body will always register Em's death and dying at this time of year. I need to honor these days. Even though I can look back and say my relationship with Em was only meant for a time, not forever, *it still hurts like hell.* I cried several times today but I have this determination now to go on, to not be stuck in the past.

Linda, on the other hand, felt that she had not made any progress at all in the two years since Tonya had died.

I have run so hard and so fast during the past two years that it is catching up with me now, especially in my obsession with my weight and my alcohol intake. Now, at two years after her death, I am almost just as miserable as I was on day one.

Everything I do is affected by losing Tonya. I cannot stand any holidays, especially Thanksgiving, Christmas, or New Year's. Try explaining that to others.

Linda was able to admit that two years later she was not coping well with the loss. In contrast, Dale noted that she still had a strong sense of Carol's presence at the second-year mark:

Even though it has been a little over two years, I find myself still talking to her in my head. I feel her presence as I again take grad classes and know she would have loved it here. I find, especially when I am down, that I talk to her. It was her unconditional love that gave my life wings.

Dale continued to feel connected to Carol even two years later. Ellen described both the ritual she created for the second anniversary of Kate's death and the meaning she found in it:

The second memorial was a way to acknowledge that it is not all gone, she is not forgotten. I needed to ritualize it. I wrote a poem and put it in the paper with her picture. I arranged a Mass. The kids and I got up together and spoke at the memorial about Kate and then sang a song together. I wanted to say—We all have loss, but what we need to do is feel it and work on it.

I had everyone light a candle and say the name of someone they had lost while my daughter slowly drummed. I called it a Ritual for Remembrance. I feel like Kate and I are still connected. One of the meanings of life is loss. We are constantly needing to be reborn. What takes the pain and turns it into life is feeling it and not denying it.

Ellen found a way to make sense of Kate's death by talking about how all of life involves loss. She took comfort in knowing that such loss is part of the death-rebirth cycle of life. In contrast, Maureen continued to sometimes experience a sense of unreality even at the second anniversary of Robin's death. She was struggling to create a new life for herself.

> At two years, I still found myself thinking some days, "Where is she?" I still look at every blue Chevy Cavalier that goes by to see if it is her. It is hard to move on because every time I go somewhere we used to go, somebody always asks, "Where is your partner?" I feel like I don't "fit" anywhere. My lesbian friends are all couples, and I feel uncomfortable being a "single." They don't have children and I have a baby, but I don't "fit" with heterosexual moms either.

Maureen had been widowed and become a mother within a few months of each other. At two years after Robin's death, she was still struggling to find a place for herself in the world. As I had done on the first anniversary, I wrote Emily a letter around the time of the second anniversary of her death:

> In some ways, this second year was worse than the first year. The pain of losing you became more real, not in the deep physical and emotional way I experienced the first year but in the reality of your absence and my need to build a life without you. Now something has shifted inside me toward you and my future.
>
> I can cherish the love we shared without regret. In our relationship, I saw you as the strong one. Now it is time for me to be strong and be fully who I am instead of thinking that I can't do it. This is the first time in my life to be completely on my own rather than living my life adjusting to other people. And yet, in that acknowledgment, there is still the appreciation that I would not be where I am today without you.
>
> I have to completely reenvision my life now. I am an older woman living on her own, having a life of her own. *And* I can be happy with that instead of feeling something is missing. It is not just that I lost you. I have a whole new life to live. I am grieving the loss of *who I was* with you.

Grief books talk about this shift in identity after we are widowed, the movement from being a "we," one-half of a couple, to being an "I," an individual (Worden, 2002). This shift from "we" to "I" was especially poignant to Pat at the second anniversary of Betty's death.

> This was a critical time for me to review our life together and to find myself outside of our relationship. For thirty-one years I had devoted myself to Betty and her family. I was still a youngster when we got together and had grown up with her. Although

I had matured, I had not developed an identity separate from Betty. My whole purpose in those years was always to make our life together as good as it could be and to help Betty get what she wanted from life.

Because I was brought up to put my personal desires secondary to those of my mate, our relationship worked well for Betty. Essentially it worked for me as well, at least until I no longer had a mate. Then I had to learn a new way of living.

Another way of living. A way of having a sense of herself as an individual with a future. That's how Pat described what she was experiencing. Heather related how she had come to realize the importance of having an identity of her own, even if she was involved in another relationship:

> I think the biggest way Ruth's death has affected me is that I consciously think about the possibility of sudden or early death, either of myself or Annie [her current partner]. I'm not willing to get lost in a relationship and disappear the way many lesbians do. I try to make sure that I always have other people actively in my life who cherish me and can provide some support and emotional intimacy if Annie dies before I do.
>
> If Annie is my life, then losing her would mean I would have nothing left. And that is not okay with me. So my friendships can be very intimate—emotionally, not sexually. At first this was hard on Annie. I remember one time during our first year together, we were visiting a friend of mine, and Annie was uncomfortable to see how the friend and I looked at one another. The intimacy in our expressions made it look like more than friendship to her. But as we spend more time together, she has understood my need and desire for more intimate friendships. I am sure it helps that our own intimacy has continued to grow.

Heather was determined to not lose herself in a relationship again, while Samantha wrote that she was aware that she still needed to "find" herself:

> I knew that it would take time to find myself again, so I spent most of the first year crying every day and being with my dog, who really was the only support that I knew I could count on.

Currently I am unemployed so I decided to take some time for myself to continue the quest of finding myself. That time will end soon, but I am thankful for having had the break. I feel more at ease with myself and more hopeful about the future. Slowly but surely I am rebuilding myself, and I feel more in touch with the spiritual side of things.

Samantha was able to give herself time to come to a new understanding of herself. Ellen expressed the shift in her identity this way: "There is no way that grief is merely a psychological state to get through. It is a complete reorientation of my life." Reorientation seems an apt word to describe what began happening for many of us in the second year after our partner's death. While our partner was alive, we were part of a couple who had plans for a future together. After her death, we had to reorient ourselves to a future without her. Although boys in our culture are socialized to be autonomous, girls tend to develop a sense of self through their relationships. The loss of a spouse by a woman, then, involves a need to redefine herself apart from what had been her primary relationship.

The experiences of the first two years after a lover's death, which I have been describing in this chapter, are consistent with grief literature that talks about adjusting to a life where the deceased partner is missing and the need to develop a new self-identity based on a life without the person who died (Worden, 2002). We must come to a sense of ourselves as unique individuals rather than identifying ourselves as part of a couple. We must create a new life for ourselves as those unique individuals.

Married women face this shift of identity too, but there seems to be a slightly different emphasis for them. Grief books that I looked through that were written for married widows included information about practical things such as handling finances or taking care of household chores (Fitzgerald, 1994). Especially for those who had been in traditional marriages and perhaps had never worked outside the home, this was a very dramatic change. They found themselves, after the death of their husband, having to take on roles formerly performed by their husband.

Of the lesbian widows who contacted me, however, not a single one mentioned that sort of difficulty. Lesbian couples, in general, tend to share tasks and roles more equally than heterosexual couples (Walter, 2003). Our struggle was to recreate ourselves emotionally for a new life without our loved one, while at the same time finding a way to maintain some kind of connection to the soul mate we had lost.

Chapter 12

Loving Again

After the first anniversary of Em's death, friends started asking me if I was dating. Dating was the furthest thing from my mind. I was still so depressed that I could not imagine being with someone else. It was all I could do to get together with friends and act sociable for a few hours. I really needed and wanted time alone. As I made new friends, I always introduced myself as recently widowed. That was how I thought of myself, and I had no interest in doing anything more than making friends with other lesbians. Marilyn felt the same way. Writing about her experience one and a-half years after Cheryl's death, Marilyn related that she was content identifying herself as a widow: "I have made a home in a new church community where I am known exactly as who I am: Mom of three, and a widow of my life partner, Cheryl."

Others, however, became involved in new relationships relatively quickly. Pat described how surprised she was to find herself attracted to someone new. It was unexpected and initially frightening for her.

> Just about a year after Betty's passing, as I was wondering what to do next with my life, an acquaintance called me and asked me to coffee. We were both very comfortable with each other, which turned out to be as unusual for her as it was for me. What happened next was totally unexpected. I found that I was physically attracted to her and was frightened by this new awakening. I did not expect anything like this to happen for years to come. I did not want to pursue my feelings. However, as we say, our bodies have a mind of their own, and we connected. I was walking on air for months after that, as we are more sexually compatible than Betty and I ever were.

Dale reported to me that, two years after Carol's death, she was involved with "a wonderful woman." Linda, on the other hand, took the risk of starting a new relationship, only to be hurt again.

A lesbian widow I met on the Internet called me one night saying she needed to escape some crap at home. She came to visit me one weekend. Over time, we struck up a friendship. In March of this year, when I saw her again, we decided that we both had feelings about each other that were more than friendship. We decided that we wanted to start a relationship. It would be difficult given our geographic disparity, my travel schedule for work, and the fact that we did not know how we would react.

Unfortunately/fortunately, it was only to last several months. The sex, of course, was great, wonderful, fascinating, and troubling all at the same time. I missed the closeness of someone next to me. I missed the human touch. For some reason still unknown to me, this friend decided on my birthday this year to dump me. I did not think I could hurt anymore after losing Tonya. However, being dumped hurt in ways I never thought possible.

Being hurt again, of course, is something that we all feared. But even if we were not hurt the way that Linda was, starting a new relationship was fraught with complications.

PROBLEMS EXPERIENCED

Ellen became involved with another woman rather quickly after Kate's death, but admitted the difficulties she experienced:

I went online to this Web site and contacted a woman who had written a poem about spring. We became lovers quickly. I learned a lot through that, but making love with her for the first time was horrible. I cried and sobbed. But it ended up being incredibly healing. We are still friends and lovers, yet I do not feel I can make the commitment I did to Kate, at least not yet.

Anita also met someone online. Writing to me about eighteen months after Holly's death, Anita disclosed that she was in a new relationship but also had a fear of being hurt again:

I met someone on the Internet. She lives in another state, so here I go with another long-distance relationship. She is younger too. I do not want my current partner to die. I want to die first. Absolutely. I am not going to go through that crap again. I can't.

But one good thing is that my present partner is out with her family and we openly show that. So that has been really nice for me. One problem is that she wants me to live with her, which is wonderful, but that means that I have to sell my home. And of course I will bring my furniture and everything with me, but that is going to be hard because I am attached here. My home has been a solace for me since Holly died.

Anita seemed to be weighing the pros and cons of moving in with her new partner. Pro—her partner was out. Con—it meant letting go of the things that had been giving her comfort and reminding her of Holly.

Lois reported that she became involved in a new relationship during the second year after Joan's death, but there were complications for her relationship also:

By two years [after Joan's death], I had met my new partner and rather precipitously moved to the country. I still do not know if it was the best thing to do; sometimes I can hardly believe I did it. But I love being in the country so much; I cannot imagine still living in the city. My partnership grows more steady all the time, though the path has not been easy. I just felt pretty clear, and still do, that life is too short to wait and see. My children have had a hard time accepting that I have chosen a partner again. They were not ready to "replace" Joan.

Lois made an important point: Even if a widow is ready for a new relationship, it may be difficult for others, in Lois's case the children, to adjust. Not all the widows who contacted me, however, became involved in relationships right away. Many waited a long time before they fell in love again. For Janet, it was thirteen years.

For years I floated along. I watched people go into relationships with all the grand ideas and never knowing what might be coming around the corner. And I knew what could come around that corner. As for myself, I learned more about what I did not want than what I did. I was content with the quality of my life, and happy that I had developed great friends to spend time with. All the while knowing that I would never love like that again.

I was resolved to not find the same relationship, but I did require the same quality in a relationship. Friends tried to help with dates and even personal ads, but I had found my perfect love and was not willing to let her go. I was quite happy being a widow. I dated and tried on relationships but knew that the one perfect love was gone.

Thirteen years after Chris died, I was content with my existence. Then she walked into my life. At my New Year's day potluck, she strolled in, and my life changed. I felt that tingling sensation again when she would call or drop by the house, and now when she comes home to me. Our relationship is different, but I found I could love as deep and as hard and as wild as I had shared with Chris. I have never tried to replace Chris, and I share with my partner how I feel. Somewhere inside I know that Chris guided Annie to me.

Janet made two significant statements. She still remembers and misses Chris. And her new partner is understanding of that. The other widows in this study who were in new relationships reported the same thing. Starting a new relationship did not mean that they forgot about their previous partner, and their new partner was supportive of the emotional connection they maintained with their deceased lover.

Heather related how difficult it was for her to love someone else even five years after Ruth's death. But her new partner, like Janet's, is also very accepting of her continued sense of connection to Ruth.

Seven years ago, five years after Ruth's death, I met a wonderful woman, and we have been together since. I knew early on that Ruth would be a hard act for anyone to follow because she was so wonderful, of course, but also because she was dead. At least if a relationship broke up, the new girlfriend can consider herself more loyal or somehow better than the last one. But how does one compete with a dead ex?

Angie [her current partner] did it by not trying. She loves me, and just seems to view Ruth as part of me and my life. For example, she never objected to the pictures I keep around, even though for at least our first couple of years I had a picture of

Ruth and myself in the bedroom, along with the picture of Angie and me.

In a similar vein, Traci's new partner is accepting of Dana's place in Traci's life. Six years after Dana's death, Traci wrote,

> I am involved in another relationship. It took me a long time to commit myself to another person. After Dana died, I dated a lot of people. I had a hard time letting Dana go. I dated, trying to forget my tragedy. My new partner encourages me to speak of Dana and does not feel threatened when I do so.

By accepting the role of Dana in Traci's life, her new partner created a bond with Traci that makes their new relationship thrive. Although Traci committed to someone new six years after Dana's death, Anna Marie did not partner with anyone until eleven years after Caroline passed away.

> It was several years before I considered dating. I would go with some of my friends to different things. I had women hit on me. This one got pretty intense and I told her I came here by myself and I am going home by myself. I felt like I would be betraying Caroline if I were to go out with somebody.
> Finally I got it together after seeing a counselor for a while. Around eleven years after Caroline's death, I again dated a few women before I met a woman at this group and we are together. She is very supportive.

Once again we hear in Anna Marie's story the theme of a new partner being supportive about the role of the deceased partner in a widow's life. When Jane shared her story with me, it was three years after Lynn had passed away. She described the tentativeness and yet the excitement of beginning a new relationship:

> One person has amazingly emerged as my possible future partner. We have been dating each other exclusively for almost a year now, and I am relearning the idea of future and a different kind of love, although it is as vital as the one I shared with Lynn.
> This love will leave more room for me as an individual, although I never really minded how I grew into an adult with

Lynn. Starting over has its lessons to take advantage of, and I am trying to look on the positive side of having been forced to start over. Yes, it would be easier to still be with Lynn, more comfortable, more what I thought my middle age into old age would be, but I am accepting this new life because I have someone to share it with.

The new relationship is exciting and frustrating. I am afraid of making comparisons, falling into habits that were habits with Lynn and might make this new person uncomfortable. Finding out how to start and continue a relationship at such a new stage with the possibilities of permanency at stake seems to carry a lot more pressure and risk than I remember a relationship having when I was younger. So we are both trying to find our way with each other. I enjoy being shown new things, and sharing my life and career with her as well.

Jane is tentatively making her way through a new experience. Joy, on the other hand, has already settled into a new relationship.

I became involved in a relationship just a few years ago that did not work out. Then I met Judy three years ago, ten years after Barbara's death. She is my life. I am her life. We live in happiness.

It was a total surprise to me when, two years after Em's death, I realized I was attracted to a woman I met at a women's music festival. I had not had that kind of feeling for any woman since Emily died. I knew I had done a lot of emotional work toward grief recovery over the previous two years and was creating a new life for myself without Emily, but I thought it would still be years before I would ever get involved with someone else.

It actually was not a very good time in my life for me to be thinking about starting a new relationship. I had moved again. I had decided that I was ready to leave the "retreat center" apartment that I lived in for two years because I felt like the worst of my grieving was over. Moving someplace new felt like an outer sign of an inner shift. However, I was barely unpacked when I found myself having to do a job search because I thought I would be losing my job at the end of the school year. Also, my oldest son, who was serving in the U.S. Army, was notified that he would be doing a tour of duty in South Korea in the coming year. That created a lot of anxiety for me too. So it really was not a good time to become involved with someone else. But I could not get Carole out of my mind.

Carole and I live in communities about a four-hour drive apart, so I initially made contact by e-mailing her. The e-mails quickly became daily and within a month or so we were admitting that we thought we were falling in love.

I just got an e-mail from Carole saying that she thinks she is falling in love with me via e-mail. Wow. Take a deep breath. I think it is reciprocal but I am scared to death. We are definitely "soul mates" or kindred spirits. It seems like this is just a crazy time to be doing this. My life is in such upheaval and my future in the air. But, on the other hand, it really resonates with me. This feels like one very positive, upbeat part of my life, much better to think about than committee work, job search, or my kids.

After continued e-mails and phone calls, we decided that, at our age, there was no point in waiting. Carole and I have now been in a committed relationship for more than three years. I felt from the beginning that I had Emily's blessing on the relationship, that perhaps she even had something to do with bringing us together. Carole does not replace Em. It is a totally different relationship, a more mature love. I have felt guilty at times when I have talked about or cried over Em when I am with her, but Carole has been wonderfully supportive. It has been interesting to realize that I can love both of them at the same time in different ways. I can be grateful for what Em and I had in the past while at the same time enjoying and appreciating the deeper, more stable relationship I have now with Carole.

Carole developed some health problems after we were together a few months. They were not life-threatening, but I still found myself fearful that I would lose her. I could not bear the thought of being widowed again; the pain would be too incredible to stand. Carole has tried to assure me that she is a fighter and plans to be around for a long time, but it is still sometimes a struggle for me not to worry about the future. The longer we are together, however, the more confident I become.

MYTHS ABOUT GRIEF

One of the myths that people tend to believe about grief is that the goal should be to get over your grief as soon as possible. Friends may tell us we should pack away her pictures or keep busy to avoid thinking about her. But the truth is that we will never get over our loss and we will never forget someone we have loved that deeply. What we do is learn to live with our grief. We change our relationship with our deceased partner to one of memory rather than one of having her physically present with us.

Some time ago, I read a letter written to an advice columnist. A man was complaining that his new wife kept talking about her first husband, who had died three years prior to her current marriage to him. The advice columnist, who was also male, agreed with the letter writer that his wife needed to quit talking about her previous husband and get on with her life. That advice is the total opposite of what the lesbian widows in this book reported to me about their new relationships. Without exception, everyone talked about their deceased partner with their new lover, and the new partner was supportive and not threatened by their continuing sense of connection with that deceased partner. I believe this ability to talk with our new partner about our deceased partner reflects two characteristics of lesbians. One is the deep sense of connection between two women, a connection that is not easily forgotten. Second is the practice in lesbian communities of including ex-lovers in one's extended network of friends. Including our departed partner in that network is just another extension of that practice.

STILL SINGLE

Not everyone will necessarily become involved in a new relationship, however. Eleven women, just under half of the lesbian widows in this book, were not involved in another relationship when they contacted me. The time ranged from six months to seven years after the death of their loved one for these eleven. Some widows, like Samantha, indicated that they felt they still needed time to be alone. "It is three years ago that Marie died. I am still single and I am still trying to figure things out for myself."

Pam and Maureen admitted that they were afraid of a new relationship. Pam wrote,

> I have not become involved in another relationship. I really needed to make peace with Sandy and her passing before I could

even consider another relationship. I must say I am really "scared" of even the idea of a new relationship.

Three years after being widowed, Maureen shared,

> I am scared to start another relationship because I know nobody will ever take her place in my heart. It is harder to move on when, at the time of her death, I could not have loved her more than I did. When you break up with someone, everyone looks better than the last loser you left or who left you, but this was so different.

I heard from Maureen again a year after I interviewed her, which would have been almost four years after Robin's death. At the time she had just given birth to twins. They joined the little girl who was born three months after Robin passed away. Maureen packed up all three children and moved across the country to be closer to her family. She e-mailed me this message: "I still have not dated since she died except one or two dinner dates. Maybe someday I will move on and date, and it will be easier not living in our house."

Typically anyone, straight or gay, who loses a partner cannot initially imagine dating or making a commitment to someone else. Eventually, though, many of us found ourselves considering it, even though we may have felt guilty or unfaithful at first for doing so. The new relationship, however, never replaces the previous one. Especially for young widows, grieving continues even after a new relationship is formed (Walter, 2003).

Chapter 13

Grief over Time

What does it mean to recover from the death of a loved one? And how quickly will it happen? These are the kinds of questions many of us asked ourselves as we continued to mourn longer than we ever thought possible. It may be easier to start with what grief recovery does *not* mean. It does not mean we will not miss our deceased partner. It does not mean we will forget her. It does not mean that we will always be upbeat and never feel pain again. It does not mean that there will not be times that we long for her and the life we had together (Rando, 1988).

What grief recovery does mean is that we have learned to live with our grief. We will never entirely stop mourning, but we will be able to think of our deceased partner without feeling emotional agony. We may not have had a choice about our partner dying, but we do have a choice about how we will let our loss affect us. After the initial time of feeling deep pain, we can choose to cherish our memories or stay bitter. We can choose to stay stuck in our grief or move forward.

As to the question, "How long does grieving take?" there is no identifiable time scale that fits everyone. There are no time limits, and no right or wrong way to mourn, although in general the pain is the worst in the first two years. At some level, we never stop grieving. In this chapter, I look at how lesbian widows talked about their grief over time. Among the twenty-four widows included in this book, there was a range of six months to seventeen years since their partner died. As we read their comments, it is clear that time, by itself, is no guarantee of recovery. Women widowed for the same amount of time were in varied places emotionally. I begin with reflections of those who contacted me within the first two years.

GRIEF IN THE FIRST TWO YEARS

Nine of the twenty-four lesbian widows, a little over one-third of those in this book, contacted me within the first two years of their partner's death, when grief tends to be most intense. After the first two years, we may still experience moments of grief, but those moments will tend to be less extreme, not last as long, and not happen as frequently.

Three women contacted me less than a year after their partner had passed away. First, let us listen to Beverly.

Beverly at Six Months

Beverly and Virginia were partners for thirty-seven years. Virginia died of cancer at age sixty-nine. Beverly was the widow in this book who had been in a committed relationship the longest, and yet the shortest amount of time had passed since her partner's death. With Virginia's death still so close, Beverly noted that she liked to stay home because that was where she could feel Virginia's presence.

> It really did help that I had some time, quite a lot of time [while Virginia was sick] to get used to the idea and try to anticipate what it would be like not having her. There are certain things that have been different than I anticipated, like trips. I thought that I would just be ready to go on trips as soon as she was gone. But here it is almost six months and I don't like to be away from the house at night. I feel close to her here at home or at places we have been. I rarely go out to her niche, which I thought I would do a lot, but I don't feel close to her there, like I do here at home or in places where we went together, and loved and enjoyed together so much.

At six months, Beverly talked about being surprised that she did not feel like following through on her plan of taking trips. Perhaps that will change over time.

Shirley at Six Months

Shirley, the other widow writing from the six-month time frame, commented on the level of pain she had experienced and wondered what the pain level would be like in the future. Shirley and Terry were partners for eleven years before Terry died suddenly and unexpectedly when Terry was thirty-eight and Shirley was fifty-four.

> I am a social worker in a nursing home in Nebraska. There is not a lot of support here for the gay/lesbian world, let alone for those who are grieving over the loss of a partner. Being a lesbian in Nebraska is very hard, but I would like to share with you how surprised I was at all the support I received when my partner died and the community realized we were a lesbian couple.
>
> I must say, this is the most difficult thing I have ever had to cope with. My friends tell me I am doing a wonderful job of grieving, as does my counselor. But it just feels good to be able to talk to someone who has experienced the loss of a partner. I have so many friends who are supportive and caring, but they have not actually experienced the loss.
>
> Some days, it is easy and almost a relief to talk about Terry and her death. On other days, I can barely think about her without such sadness, let alone talk about her. When Terry first died and I was so distraught, I wondered if I would feel differently at the six-month mark. Would the pain be less? Would I hurt so much? Would I cry so easily?
>
> Now that the sixth month is approaching, I know the answers to those questions. The pain is still there, but not in the depth it was before. I still hurt, but it does not last as long. I still cry, but not as easily or as often or as intensely. Now I wonder about the one-year mark. What will that bring?
>
> I imagine that any day or date connected with me and Terry is going to have some sort of impact upon me. My prayer would be that the impact become less as time goes on.

If we allow ourselves to mourn in a healthy way, then the pain will lessen over time, just as Shirley predicted, even though, in the beginning, it is hard to imagine how that could be possible.

Vera at Eight Months

Vera was another widow who responded to my questionnaire within the first year after her partner's death. Vera was together with

Nancy for sixteen years. They were forty-five and fifty-four, respectively, when Nancy died from cancer. Vera spoke of feeling connected to others and of being at peace with Nancy's death.

> Over the summer I realized that there were actually some times that I felt good. Not wonderful but good. Other days when I was just okay. What I have learned since Nancy's death is how connected we all are. I felt really disconnected during Nancy's illness a lot of the time. Not from Nancy, although sometimes from her too, but more so from other people. I don't really feel that way anymore. I just feel like there is this huge loving web of connection that I am part of and that has been very comforting and reassuring.
>
> Nancy will always be in my heart for the rest of my life. I feel I have made peace with her death. I feel that her death was a blessing. If I were waving a magic wand, she would be alive and healthy, but I could never have asked that she stay alive longer when she was beginning to be in pain and would have had to have kidney dialysis. That would have totally changed the quality of her life. It has been almost eight months since her death and I am still here.

At eight months, Vera had good days and bad days, taking comfort in knowing that Nancy would suffer no more and that she will always be in Vera's heart. I liked her statement, "I am still here." Still being here feels like an accomplishment after the crushing pain we experienced.

Marilyn and Anita wrote at approximately one and one-half years after their partner's death. Let us listen to Marilyn first.

Marilyn at Twenty Months

Marilyn and Cheryl had lived together for thirty-one years. Thirty-one years in the closet. Their lives revolved around three adopted children with disabilities and their work in the handicapped community. After a long, difficult illness, Cheryl died at age fifty-seven from ALS.

> I will never go back into the closet, but I don't know if I will find another love. It is awfully complicated. Maybe if we had been a

part of the GLTB scene before, it would be a little easier. Or maybe I am just not ready. Or maybe too scared of having to choose between a new love and my kids. That is work for the future. Meanwhile it is now twenty months since Cheryl's death. There are more good days then bad, but many long nights.

Like Vera at eight months, Marilyn spoke of having good times and bad times at twenty months.

Anita at Twenty Months

Anita indicated that she had made peace with Holly's death, yet there is still a sense of disbelief that Holly could have died so suddenly, along with a certain amount of bitterness at Holly's brother. Holly and Anita were in a commuter relationship for eight and one-half years before Holly died at age fifty-four.

> I have made peace with her death, but I still have not gotten over what her brother did. His shunning me, ostracizing me, selling her house without telling me, auctioning all her furniture, everything, including my stuff. I mean, how dare he? I have learned to make the most of each day because you really never know. Holly was never sick, never missed a day at work. She was a smoker and she drank. But who knew? Who knew?

Four women (Dale, Linda, Nora, and Ellen) wrote about their experiences two years after the death of their partner. Each was in a slightly different place emotionally. Dale spoke of dull acceptance of death; Linda was cynical; Nora expressed gratitude; and Ellen was philosophical.

Dale at Two Years

Dale and Carol were partners for fourteen years, seven in which they lived together, and seven in which Dale visited Carol daily in a nursing home. Carol died in Dale's arms from MS at the age of sixty-one.

> Carol has now been dead for two years and it just seems like yesterday. I sold the house we had owned together and that was difficult. I don't know how exactly one makes peace with death. I think there is just a dull acceptance.

Linda at Two Years

While Dale had reached some level of acceptance, Linda was clearly still in pain. Linda and Tonya were together for two and one-half years before Tonya died from complications from gastric bypass surgery. She was only thirty-eight years old. Linda became involved in a new relationship after Tonya's death, but shortly before she contacted me, she had been dumped. She was bitter about that experience as it only magnified the unresolved pain of Tonya's death.

> What I have learned from all this is to never get into a relation-ship again, never let anyone get that close again and never, never let anyone near my heart again. I also want to do whatever I can to help others avoid this kind of pain.

Most likely, in time and perhaps with some help, Linda will be able to heal her hurt and allow herself to love again.

Nora at Two Years

Nora and Anne were lovers for only five months before Anne died from cancer, but their sense of connection was so profound that Nora was deeply affected.

> Sometimes I regret that I do not feel emotions intensely any-more, at least for now, but I would rather have that than experi-ence the pain and rage I had before. Anne was a gift. It was the first time I truly felt love for someone without any regrets for the past or any unfulfilled longing for the future. As Virginia Woolf would have put it, it was "a moment of being."

Nora was glad that the pain had lessened. Despite the pain, she spoke of having no regrets for what had happened.

Ellen at Two Years

Ellen described how painful the first year was and then spoke rather philosophically of her experience two years after Kate's death.

The first year was wide-open raw. My spiritual director said the second six months were harder. It breaks into your consciousness. Reality sinks in. You are really never going to see her again. The sorrow comes and goes in powerful ways. Like intense labor. The first half of the first year I was in shock; the second half was deciding to be here. Am I going to make the choice to live again?

This is excruciatingly painful. Way more than others acknowledge. Everybody wants you to move on quickly. For them four months was a long time. The idea that this is a process that takes weeks and months is ridiculous. Actually, it takes years and it gets incorporated into your life.

You have to go through it, not deny it. You have to feel the depth of it. This other woman, her way of coping was to keep extremely busy to distract herself, but I cannot see how that works. You cannot get out of it. The whole point of it is that people die. This is the way the world works. We are all going to die. I have that with me as my teacher.

Ellen related, in her own words, what grief books tell us: You have to feel the pain before you can heal. If you avoid it, you will only hurt yourself and never fully recover.

As we read the comments of those widows who shared their stories within two years or less since their partner's death, there is an overall sense of pain easing over time, although Anita was still angry at Holly's brother, and Linda was bitter about being hurt again.

AROUND THREE YEARS

Seven of the widows included in this book wrote to me around the three-year anniversary of their partner's death. Some were still struggling emotionally but most seemed to have made some kind of peace with being widowed.

Pat and Maureen both contacted me two and one-half years after the death of their partner. Pat was already involved in another relationship and felt she had a better understanding of herself as a result of the grief work that she had done. Maureen, on the other hand, was still grieving and afraid of dating someone else.

Pat at Two and One-Half Years

Pat and Betty lived together for thirty-two years before Betty died from cancer at age fifty-four. Pat "grew up" with Betty and never really developed a sense of identity apart from her. Since Betty's death, she has worked on getting to know herself better.

> Looking back on our relationship has made me approach my new relationship differently. I do not think that I will ever give myself up so completely again. That is not to suggest that I am not committed to my new relationship, only that I have learned to create boundaries so that I do not lose myself in the relationship. For all the loving years that Betty gave me, I will always be grateful. I will always try to honor her memory by being a person of whom she would be proud.

Although she was focusing on finding herself and having better boundaries in future relationships, Pat still was connected to Betty and did not regret the years of her life with her. She wanted Betty to be proud of her. I think that Pat wanting to make Betty proud of her is similar to feelings I have had about Emily. It was with Em's support and encouragement that I began a new career as a college professor. When she died, I really missed having her to talk with about student or faculty problems, and I missed hearing her remind me that I could succeed in this new profession. Over time, however, I adopted the image of Emily dropping her mantle of teaching skills over my shoulders, as if I had inherited them from her. I discovered from other research that this was a common thing for lesbians to do, to incorporate some of the positive characteristics of their deceased partners into their own personalities (Walter, 2003).

Maureen at Two and One-Half Years

Maureen was thirty-four and pregnant when Robin died of breast cancer. Two and one-half years after Robin's death, she wrote,

> I am still working in a clinic where there are a lot of patients going through chemo, and I find it hard sometimes to even look at the women. Sometimes someone will have a bald head and it will catch me off guard.

I am not sure I have made peace with her death. I guess if I felt like I had, maybe I would feel like I could date again or talk about her without crying. Some days are worse and some are not that bad.

This has been such a learning experience for me to do this questionnaire. I laughed when I remembered the good times; I cried when I thought about how devastated we were when we found out about the return of the cancer. I realized how much work I still have to do, and I thought about how much I really did love and what I lost.

Maureen thought she really had not come to terms with Robin's death yet. She found that she still had difficult days and was still quite aware of her sense of loss.

Four women contacted me exactly three years after their partner's death. Their responses reflect that they too were in different places in their grief recovery even though they were writing from the same time frame. Irene and Samantha seemed to have made some sense of their experience while Pam was afraid of being in another relationship and Jane was still struggling with what happened. Let us begin with Irene.

Irene at Three Years

Irene and MJ were partnered for twenty years. MJ died of cancer when she was fifty-one years old.

Now, at the third anniversary, I'm finally feeling I am starting to heal in a way I have not up until now. I do not believe we heal with time. Time only steals from us our close connection to what was before. We lose part of what we felt and even more of what we remember. This makes a difference in how we feel in time. It takes the edge off of our grief, but it is sad to lose the close connection because there is a comfort in grieving, albeit a painful comfort.

It feels less painful to me now to be without MJ, but it also feels sad, a new grief to know part of my connection to her is gone. It is changing and I cannot stop that from happening. My sorrow is less over what was lost for us and more for myself. It is a new sadness, but one I can do something about. I can do things for myself to change this. I can do nothing to change what happened to MJ. I am starting to understand it as "the will to go on." It feels doable like nothing else felt through all of my grieving to this point.

Irene, at three years after MJ's death, made a comment similar to Nora's, two years after Anne's death, that there was a sense of losing the close connection to her deceased partner as the pain eased. This is a normal part of grief recovery. Over time, however, we come to a place where we realize that we do not have to feel pain to stay connected. We can find a new place for our loved one in our heart, a place where we cherish our memories of her and of our time together in such a way that it is no longer so painful.

Irene made another important point. "My sorrow is less over what is lost for us and more for myself." She was making a shift from being focused on thinking about the past, when she was part of a couple, to realizing that she must now create a new future for herself alone. A third key point she made was about the importance of being involved in our own grief recovery process. Time alone does not heal; we must actively participate in order to heal.

Samantha at Three Years

Samantha, at three years, wrote about the spiritual side of her experience. Samantha and Marie lived together for five years before Marie died of cancer.

> I am still in the process of recovery even though it has been three years, but the future looks brighter as time inevitably continues to pass. Slowly but surely I am rebuilding myself, and I feel more in touch with the spiritual side of things. Neither Marie nor myself bought into organized religion, but I think that we both believed deeply in spirituality and the basic bottom-line ideology of all religions. My hope is that I have learned to be a kinder and more accepting individual, less judgmental of others and myself. I do not get out much, so it is clear that, on some level, I am still afraid of involvement, but I am still trying, and for that I give myself credit.

I like how Samantha said, "I am still trying, and for that I give myself credit." She saw this traumatic experience as a pathway to personal growth. This is similar to Vera's comment, eight months after Nancy's death, "I am still here." There is something to be said for just surviving this life-altering experience that was not of our choosing.

Pam at Three Years

Pam and Sandy were partnered for ten years. Pam was forty when Sandy died from cancer. She shared how her grief has changed over the past three years.

> It has now been a little over three years since Sandy died. I am no longer so massively depressed. I am still sad and miss her every day. But it is not the kind of missing where I thought that, if I missed her enough and thought about her enough, she would come back.
>
> I have never hidden my relationship with Sandy or the fact that I am a lesbian from anyone. I am not ashamed of it. Instead, I celebrate it. Sandy is gone and I will always miss her. But I also know that it is time to move on with my life. I have not become involved in another relationship. I really needed to make peace with Sandy and her passing before I could even consider another relationship. I must say I am really "scared" of even the idea of a new relationship.

There was clearly a shift for Pam from deep depression when Sandy died to three years later, where she missed Sandy but not in such a painful way. Pam knew it was time to move ahead in her life but was afraid of what that might mean and what a new relationship might bring. These are all very normal feelings, all part of the grief recovery process.

Jane at Three Years

Twenty-three years together ended for Jane and Lynn when Lynn died of cancer at age fifty-one. In their years together, Jane and Lynn shared a love of dance and teaching dance. Jane was widowed at age forty-four and wrote of how she continued to struggle with Lynn's death, even after three years. She still seemed to be blaming herself.

> Lynn has been dead for almost three years. It is hard to say that. Some days it feels like yesterday; some days it seems impossible I had such a relationship for so many years of my life.

I am *always* surprised at what still bothers me about the loss of her, the memories of the death itself, my regrets, even surprised at the progress I feel I have made. I cannot say I will *never* understand the death, but even today (literally) I am disappointed in the lack of information I got from doctors, blaming it on myself for not asking the right questions, being too afraid to ask the questions that *did* occur to me, and wondering what I failed to do that might have changed the outcome.

Feeling guilty about a lover's illness and death is normal, but it is important not to stay stuck in those feelings. Jane might need help to let go of this guilt so that she can stop blaming herself and heal.

FOUR TO SEVEN YEARS

Five women contacted me between four and seven years after their lover's death. In their stories you can sense that, although they still remember and miss their deceased partner, they have arrived at an emotional place where life is meaningful once again.

Lois at Four Years

Lois and Joan shared nineteen years with each other before Joan died of cancer at age forty-five. Lois related the changes she has made since Joan's death. She and her family seem to have incorporated an awareness of Joan into their daily living experience. There is also a strong spiritual theme in what she shared.

At four years, I hardly ever feel overwhelmed by grief anymore. Losing Joan, however, remains a central motif of my life. It has completely changed my life. I am more fearful, more honest, more anxious, less patient, more spiritual. I have moved 250 miles, urban to rural, and become self-employed.

In February, my daughter quite unexpectedly got pregnant, and in September, my new granddaughter was born. Her name is Laynie Jonae, derived from my middle name, Elaine, and Joan. My older granddaughter, now ten, has made plans for what she will teach Laynie about her namesake: to always take care of animals, to make up songs, to dance funny, and to be a Neon Girl.

I think Lois quite nicely expressed what place the loss of our life partner will always have in our lives: "Losing Joan remains a central motif of my life." Even as we find meaning once again and the pain recedes, the death of our life partner will forever remain an essential part of how we define ourselves.

Cassie at Five Years

Cassie and Fran had been together only nine months when Cassie woke one morning to find that Fran had died in her sleep. Cassie wrote of her gratitude for even the short amount of time she had with Fran.

> I thank the Universe every morning that Fran floated through my life, and for giving me the gift of her love and light. I consider myself very fortunate that I felt totally loved by Fran. She enriched those nine months of my life.

Whether their relationship lasted five months or over thirty years, one of the ways that the widows in this book made peace with their partner's death was by being grateful for the time they had together rather than being bitter that it did not last longer.

Rose at Six Years

Like Cassie, Rose spoke of her gratitude at having been loved, even if only for a brief moment in time. Rose was forty-six and Steph was forty-two when Steph passed away. They had been together for four years.

> It has now been almost six years since Steph's death. I think I have made peace with her death, but I still think of her often and remember and cherish our time together. Mostly I remember the good times, but the hard times come back too.
> I will forever be grateful to her for helping me to come out and get that part of my life on track. She loved me in a way and with a depth that I had not experienced before, and that love changed the core of my being.

I can really identify with Rose's comment about how she was loved by Steph. Emily loved me in a way I had never been loved before, and that love changed me irrevocably. Nothing that happens in the future will change that.

Traci at Six Years

Traci and Dana were both forty-six years old when Dana died from cancer. They had lived together for sixteen years. Traci described the ups and downs, forward and backward progress of her grief journey:

> The grief journey continues every day. It is a process that does diminish with time. However, time does *not* heal all wounds! This wound will never go away! Rather she will have a special place inside of me, never to be forgotten! The entire experience was the *worst* thing I have ever had to go through!
>
> My life was stopped when Dana died, but I had to make sure it started again. My journey was one of small steps, always trying to move forward. Occasionally I slip backward; I get sad again. As time marches on, my backward steps are fewer and fewer. I wake up in the morning, grateful to be alive!

The emotional places that Traci described are all part of mourning. Traci related her gratitude just to be alive. This, too, is part of our recovery, to enjoy life once again. But it is a choice that we must make. We can choose to heal and find new joy in living, or we can choose to remain depressed, bitter, and guilty.

Donna at Seven Years

Donna shared the gratitude she felt for having known Randi:

> How often do any of us meet a soul mate? How often are two soul mates who met free of other emotional commitments and able to live together, work together, play together, and love together?
>
> This has happened in my life and provides me with a sense of awe, wonder, and immense gratitude. These feelings are tantamount, above even the sense of grief, loss, and anger at the death of my soul mate seven years ago. Yes, miracles do happen—miracles

being beneficial events, which are unexpected, unpredicted, unearned, and unlikely.

Most of the widows writing four to seven years after the death of their life partner spoke of their gratitude for having been loved and for having had the privilege of spending part of their life with their deceased partner. That does not mean it was not the most painful experience they have ever faced or that they would want to go through it again. But having lived through it, they made peace, made sense of it by being grateful for the time they had with their departed loved one.

AFTER TEN YEARS

Four women contacted me more than ten years after the death of their partner. I think this speaks to how deeply they were affected by their partner's death as well as how much they wanted to help others by sharing their story.

Heather at Twelve Years

Heather was only twenty-nine years old when Ruth died of complications from diabetes. She was widowed at the youngest age of anyone in this book. She and Ruth had lived together for seven years at the time of Ruth's death. Ruth's death has affected how Heather thinks about her own future.

> It has been twelve years now since Ruth died. I feel I have made peace with her death, and probably did so very soon after she died. I remember at some point during her last year, when she was so sick, her friend Rachel expressed her anguish at watching Ruth "die bit by bit." As a result, after that last year, her death did not feel so unwelcome.
>
> Now I sometimes am aware of when it is her birthday, our anniversary, or the anniversary of her death, and sometimes I do not notice until the date has passed. I still cry sometimes when I think or talk of her, but I do not mind. Although it still hurts, it does not hurt too much anymore. And I do not want it to ever stop hurting at all, because I always want to remember her enough to miss her sometimes.

I believe that Heather reiterated an important point. The goal is never to forget or get over our deceased loved one. It is to cherish our memories of her and the life we shared.

Joy at Thirteen Years

Joy lost Barbara to cancer after sharing two brief years of being together. She is now happy in another relationship and reflected back on the time since Barbara's death.

> It has now been thirteen years since Barbara's death. There is no pain now, just wonderment. I now feel that I gained much from our love and learned many other important things. I have made peace with her death, but only through several years of thought-provoking questions that slowly were answered.

Like Joy, we all have to find our own answers and make some kind of meaning of our experience. We all have to choose to live and go on.

Anna Marie at Fifteen Years

Anna Marie was forty-five years old when her partner Caroline died of cancer. They had been together a total of seven years.

> It has been fifteen years. It was an experience I will never forget, I know that. I think I have made peace with her death. It has been hard trying to answer this questionnaire. I guess it brings up a lot of old memories and feelings you had, but I hope that this will put this all to rest now because I have done this.

Even fifteen years later, Anna Marie admitted that remembering Caroline's death was difficult. We can learn to be happy once again, but the fact is that our lives will never be the same as they were before our partner's death.

Janet at Seventeen Years

Janet and Chris shared eight years together before Chris was shot and killed in the line of duty as a police officer. Janet was only thirty years old at the time she was widowed. Of the twenty-four women whose stories are included in this book, the greatest amount of time has passed since her partner's death, seventeen years. Her new partner is Annie.

> It has been seventeen years since Chris's death and I love my life now. Valentine's Day is still hard, but I make every effort not to show Annie, my partner, the side which misses Chris. She allows me the space. Now I let Annie know that sometimes it is okay to be sad. I have never tried to replace Chris. I share with Annie how I feel and somewhere inside I know Chris guided Annie to me. I know my mother and Chris are my angels and watch over me.

Our stories demonstrate how grief changed over time and yet also how each one of us was on a unique timetable. Some were still struggling with anger, bitterness, or fear of a new relationship. But, over time, the majority found ways to create a new life for themselves that honored the memory of their deceased partner. Quite a few widows spoke of the gratitude they felt for having had the opportunity to love and be loved by their deceased partner.

Appreciating what we had together rather than focusing on the pain of loss is one way that we recover and go on with our lives. Another way we heal over time is in discovering happiness in our new life. Finding happiness in the presence of grief seems an impossible task in the beginning. The pain is too deep. We are so focused on our tremendous loss that we lose sight of the fact that we have memories and treasures that will forever be ours. One of the most useful things I learned at the grief support group I attended was to ask myself, "What do I get to *keep*?" This helped shift my focus from what I had lost to the gift hidden in the experience.

THE GIFT IN THE GRIEVING

What follows in this section is a list of what the widows in this book identified as the gifts they received from the experience of being widowed. If we had been given a choice, none of us would have chosen to go through this experience. But, looking back, we were able to acknowledge what we had learned as a result. I start with Ellen, who wrote about the importance of finding this gift and not missing it:

For those who have grief from a person dying, the gift of this experience is there. Underneath the pain, there is something else. But if you do not face your grief, you lose the gift. The gift comes from the loss, so do not miss it! Life is about loss. Life is beautiful and horrible at the same time. One of the meanings of life is loss. We are constantly needing to be reborn. What takes the pain and turns it into life is feeling it and not denying it.

Living in the Present Moment

One gift mentioned by many widows was to realize the importance of living each day fully because there is no guarantee of having a tomorrow. Anita wrote,

> From going through this, I have learned to make the most of every day. You never know. And that is hard because sometimes you face issues and you think, "Well, I will settle it tomorrow," or "I've got next week to do this," or whatever. That is just a natural feeling. We have to know there is a future—otherwise what would happen to the universe? But what we need to do is appreciate everything that you have today.

Dale commented , "In hindsight what I have learned from the experience of losing a partner is to give all the love you can and do not put off until tomorrow what you can enjoy today." Irene expressed it this way:

> My life will always be affected by this experience. It makes me grateful for what I have had in my life and makes me realize what is truly worth worrying about and what holds no weight. It makes me understand how fragile life is and how short, and that sometimes we do not get to decide how we will go about our next day. It makes me know that love is a divine gift and that it comes in its own way, and it will not stay if you do not treasure it and respect it for what it is, and give of yourself what it deserves.
> Most of all I have learned that while we cannot know what comes of us once we leave here, we can believe what we want about whether there is anything next for us. While I would like to believe that there is more, I am satisfied to find, through this experience, that I have a spiritual side to myself that harbors me here and now regardless of what may be next. I have come to know

that this part of myself matters, and it makes me part of what it means to be human, and it connects me to all life and to something larger, unknowable and divine.

Samantha reflected on her experience:

> I never thought I would go through such an experience until I was quite a bit older, but what I have learned is that life is short and that anything can happen at any time. So enjoy what you can while you can. Value it and celebrate it whenever possible.
>
> I have also learned that control is an illusion. Going after goals and trying to attain them is fine, but you have to be flexible because, if you think you have any real control over where you end up, you are sorely mistaken.
>
> Finally, say what you feel now because you might not get the chance later. I feel fortunate that Marie and I had some time to make our peace with one another. I know that people who die in accidents or unexpectedly do not always get that chance. I was able to let Marie know that, no matter what, I loved her. I think that she finally got it in the end.

Jane stressed that, having lost a loved one, one cannot take life for granted anymore:

> I try to live each day more like I might not get another chance. That means taking some risks, and it also means being careful too. Finding more balance and *paying attention* to things said, done, and needing to be attended to is important to me now.

Traci noted the importance of appreciating good health:

> The most important lesson I have learned from my loss is that appreciating life *every* moment is of the utmost importance. Having good health is taken for granted by many people. Not by me though! I grieved while Dana was sick, after she died, and even now.

Anna Marie expressed her regret:

> I guess in hindsight I would say that I have learned that, if your lover is really ill and they want to do something, do it. Caroline

had wanted to go to Alaska, and I thought, "No, where am I going to get the money? How am I going to get off work?" But I should have done it. That is the only thing I regret I guess, not taking her and going to Alaska. Her doctor was not crazy about her going far. But I still wished I would have done it. For her.

The women whose stories are in this book were widowed at an age when one is usually not thinking about or facing mortality. Having a partner die forced us to face the fact that no one has a guarantee of a tomorrow.

Inner Strength

Another lesson we learned from our grief experience was how incredibly strong we are. As I reflected on my life and my time with Emily, I came to realize that I have much more inner strength than I ever thought I had. When Em was alive, I always thought of her as the stronger one. But it takes incredible inner strength to do grief work. In a sense, I am a survivor—I have survived the death of my lover and soul mate. Vera, likewise, talked about her resilience:

> I have learned how resilient I am. I have always known that, but I see it now ever more so. I guess that is just how I am. I have learned what a great capacity to love I have. I knew that anyway, but I still love her so much. I understand that will be with me for the rest of my life, and I would not really want it not to be, even if I end up in a relationship with another woman.

Pam also noted her surprise at realizing her inner strength and pointed out the amazing sense of being loved that she had experienced:

> What I learned from losing Sandy was how strong I really am and how much I am loved and cared about by my friends and my community. I wish she had never gotten sick and died, but for those ten years, I know I was loved and cherished in a way that no one else had ever done for me in my life. And, as far as I can see now, that is a pretty amazing thing to get from anyone. To this day, her love and devotion in the face of familial disapproval astonishes me.

Pam spoke of two main gifts she received from her grief experience: That she was strong and that she was loved; loved by Sandy but also loved by her friends. That was a significant learning experience for me too, to realize that I was loved and supported by both old and new friends. My old friends stood by me while Em was dying and supported me after her death. My new friends have listened to me talk about Em and helped me learn that I am a valuable person on my own without needing to be part of a couple. I have been amazed at the sense of being loved and supported throughout this process not only by friends but, in a spiritual sense, by the Universe. Lois touched on her sense of spiritual comfort:

> What have I learned? Humility in the face of great mystery, gratitude for the simplest things, trusting my intuition and my friends. Life really is short. I signed up for Mystery School 2002 between Christmas and New Year's when I found myself in a deep funk. I was thinking that some structure for continuing to work on Joan's death and doing spiritual work would help. I dedicated to Artemis, a paradoxical figure who is both a death bringer and a guardian of birthing.

A Different Perspective

Heather stressed how she learned to plan ahead and not act as if she would live forever. Even though she is still relatively young, she found that the experience of being widowed has given her a different perspective on life than her contemporaries.

> The primary thing I learned while Ruth was sick and I was anticipating her death was that I must do what I can to be prepared for other losses. I am a cautious person, and prepare for the future. But most days, and always when important decisions come up, I am aware that I may not be around for as long as I expect. I do not want to gamble everything on a future that may not come, or may not be what I have expected.
>
> I try to deal with this not by holding back (although I am sure I do that some), but by balancing things differently than others my age might. Most people struggle at least some with delaying gratification. I know I do. But apart from that, I find I cannot make future-oriented decisions (how much to save for retire-

ment, for example) without asking myself "what if" questions about the future. I hope to live another half century or so. But if not, I do not want to be plagued with the feeling that many of the choices I made turned out to be wrong ones.

Honoring One's Own Life

Another gift of grief learned by some of us was the necessity of taking care of ourselves and not totally losing ourselves in our relationships. Pat wrote,

> The biggest thing I have learned from losing Betty is that I have to take care of myself first. I now understand that I have to be myself, and that taking care of me is not being selfish. It is essential. I have also had an opportunity to reconnect with my own family and I do not intend to lose that again.

Jane felt she had learned the hard way that she must live her own life.

> The lessons I have learned have been those which seem unfair to learn, especially at a young age and between two people who made such an effort to make a loving life together. It is hard to accept that such talent and intelligence are taken before they have a chance to really flourish; although I find many people unexpectedly tell me how wonderfully affected they were by her.
>
> It is hard to leave her legacy to be found by those looking, but I cannot continue *her* life's work and still pursue my own. I feel as though I will keep up the dancing connection, and perhaps it will be stronger later in my life than it is now. I am trying to remain open to that and would welcome it. The learning and living process continues, and I try to find the joy and wonderment of it all.

Through our painful experiences, we discovered how to value ourselves in a new way. We learned to treasure who we are, whether or not we are in a relationship.

Altruism

For the women in this book, there was another gift: the desire to reach out and help other lesbians who were widowed. That was the reason all twenty-five of us participated in this project. Janet explicitly stated her goal of serving the lesbian community: "I am now a personal coach and life trainer and help people who have lost a loved one. I serve the community with what support I can. Doing this has helped me to grow and become human again."

Likewise, Linda spoke of her altruistic desire to help others even though she herself was not emotionally in a very good place:

> I have learned that the experience I now have needs to be shared with others. I need to be available for other lesbians who have lost their partners because I do not want them to feel as absolutely alone as I have over the past two years.

Regardless of what pain we were in ourselves or how long it was since our partner died, each of us in this book had the desire to spare others the isolation and invisibility that we experienced. Joy emphasized the importance of living life in a meaningful way. Although she went through a brief period of time after Barbara's death in which she contemplated suicide, she now has a strong sense of wanting to live in a way that will help others.

> I came to realize that suicide is the last thought to even allow into my head during hard times. Instead, I should allow others to offer their caring efforts. Most importantly, I learned that life goes on, and I have a responsibility to live and be of help to others.

Staying Open to Life

One last gift to mention from our grief experiences was explained by Rose. She spoke of not withdrawing or holding back from life or love as a result of this painful experience, but rather learning to stay open to life:

> One of the things I realized very shortly after her death is that, despite how much I hurt at losing her, the answer was *not* to avoid loving again. That, in order to experience love, I had to stay open to the possibility of pain. That is a trade-off I never would have considered viable before.
>
> Another lingering, probably permanent, effect of Steph's death is that I have a whole new appreciation for how much a

person can hurt. I thought I had hurt before in my life, but this was a whole new dimension. Fortunately, with it I also learned that healing does follow. Eventually.

It seems appropriate to end on this note. This was the most painful experience we have ever had. But healing can come. Not right away. But eventually. That is the message we wish to pass on to those who unfortunately follow in our footsteps.

Chapter 14

For Friends and Family

The more you educate yourself about grief and mourning, the more helpful you are likely to be to your lesbian friend or family member who has been widowed. Since there are many myths and misconceptions about grief, it is important that you avoid saying and doing things that are unintentionally hurtful. It is also imperative that you realize that your friend or family member needs your assistance to recover. Grief recovery does not happen alone. Our culture expects people to be happy, and we do not know what to say or how to respond to people who are grieving. You may want to "fix" her. You cannot. There is no quick fix to grief.

GRIEF TAKES TIME

Caring for your widowed friend or family member also needs to include an understanding that grieving takes time. Her pain and tears may make you feel uncomfortable, especially as they continue over time, but you must find a way to tolerate her tears if you are going to be a support rather than a hindrance. Although the pain will be most intense in the beginning, years later she may still be recycling through her grief. Grief does not follow a predictable path. One grief book likened grief to a ride on a roller coaster (Davidson and Doka, 1999). There are ups and downs, highs and lows. "Like many roller coasters, the ride tends to be rougher in the beginning, the lows deeper and longer. Gradually, though, over time the highs and lows become less intense" (p. 9). You can consult other books on grief, such as those listed in the bibliography and Appendix B of this book, as well as contacting your local hospice for more information about mourning and grief.

ACCEPT THE RELATIONSHIP

Besides understanding grief, straight family members and friends need to accept that a committed lesbian relationship is as meaningful and valued to its partners as a marriage between a man and a woman. And a lesbian whose partner dies is truly a widow, a widow who experiences the same kind of pain as her heterosexual counterpart. Women, in general, experience relationships and grieve the loss of those relationships in a very emotionally intense way. The death of her partner results in the lesbian widow feeling that not only has she lost her partner, she has also lost part of herself, as well as the future they had planned together.

The support of friends and family is vital for the lesbian widow, especially in the light of society's lack of acknowledgment of both her relationship and her state of widowhood. Therefore, when friends whom these widows thought they could count on failed to come through, it was very upsetting. Nora, for example, wrote, "Most unhelpful in my grieving were people whom I thought I could depend on who were simply not there." "Being there" is probably the most essential way you can support us. Wolfelt (1992) wrote, "Your friend may relate the same story about the death over and over again. Listen attentively each time. Realize that this repetition is part of your friend's healing process. Simply listen and understand" (p. 183). You do not have to "do something." Listening is the "doing" that is needed.

AVOID CLICHÉS

Another piece of advice that we have for those who wish to support us is that, along with just listening to us, avoid pat answers, clichés, and religious platitudes. Nora, for example, complained, "People who told me to keep my chin up were not helpful. There are times when you just hurt, and you need to be able to say that without someone feeling they can fix the problem."

If you make comments such as, "You need to move on with your life," it feels to us like you are invalidating our feelings, as if you are trying to take them away from us. These comments are not only insensitive; they increase our level of pain. Telling us to get over it makes it feel like you are telling us to forget about our loved one. We will never forget. Our lover and the time we had together will forever be part of our lives. Also, even though the contributors to this book found that their pain decreased over time, knowing that does not ease the pain a widow feels at first. Just be a witness to her pain. For all of us whose stories are in this book, losing our life partner was the most incredibly painful experience of our lives.

Contrary to the admonition to get on with our lives, we need a period of time to hold onto the person who has died. This includes time to talk to her, dream about her, and treasure possessions she gave us, as well as talking about her with others. Wilder (1998) explained, "Although these rituals may evoke pain, they also value the person who has died, and focus on . . . her life rather than solely on death and loss" (p. 205).

WHAT DOES NOT HELP

Two lesbian widows made comments specifically about religious people whom they found offensive. Ellen wrote,

> Some of the worst people were people who considered themselves religious or spiritual. One older woman at the funeral said, "God must have really wanted her in heaven." This was her explanation. Another spiritual woman told me to not cling, that I needed to move on—just a few weeks after the funeral. And all I could think was, "You don't know what the fuck you are talking about."

Nora also complained about religious people. "Also unhelpful were people who talked about miracles; it was just such a phony sense of hope." Years ago, as I was flipping television channels, I came across a well-known evangelist who was telling people that, although his mother or father (I cannot remember which) had just died, he was not going to grieve because it was the devil who wanted him to grieve. God wanted him to celebrate. I was appalled at the time and am even more so now. We need to grieve. Even if such advice is cloaked in religious language, it is not helpful. Ellen explained how she now expresses sympathy to others when a loved one has died:

> When I talk now to others who have lost a loved one, I acknowledge, "I do not know what you are going through. All I can do is

be a loving witness to your pain." Otherwise it diminishes your pain. It is a missing of the person, a shattering of the world as you knew it. It is losing your sense of control of the world. But life is transitory and we have no control of it.

Ellen's point is that even those of us who have experienced being widowed cannot say to another widow that we know exactly how she feels. Everyone's pain, everyone's story is unique. Just be with us. Just listen.

Another unhelpful thing an acquaintance said to me, in what sounded to me like an accusatory tone of voice, was, "What are you doing to take care of yourself?" I thought to myself, "Why not offer to support me instead of criticizing me?" In contrast, my friend Juanita told me that when her husband died, one woman she did not even know all that well called her every evening for the first few months, just to make sure she was okay, and how much that meant to her. Ellen mentioned how one friend just showed up to check on her for the first few months, and Pam talked about Sandy's friend Mary stopping by on a regular basis (Chapter 9).

Offering to do practical things for the widow is a good way to express that you care. Friends took me to lunch, went on walks with me, helped me move. Nora related how the most helpful people for her were those who did practical things like grocery shopping. Don't wait for us to ask. We may not even know what we need. Instead, offer to do something. But be sure you follow through.

Although lesbian friends were an important resource for the lesbian widows in this book, fellow lesbians did some things that were very hurtful. Nora related how Anne's previous partner took over sorting through Anne's personal belongings and shut her out. Ellen talked about how friends did not acknowledge her at Kate's memorial service and how upsetting that was for her (Chapter 8). Jane pointed out another problem area—a friend who made unwanted sexual advances toward her. She described her negative experience this way:

> Another friend who was actually more interested in trying to restart an affair came to visit, turning a week into a disaster. That certainly told me I would rather be alone than deal with that kind of "love." But I felt I would never be held or my hair tenderly stroked again.

HOW FRIENDS CAN HELP

In contrast to Jane's experience, Irene identified some of the things that friends provided that were really helpful to her:

> What helped was being with single friends who understood that being alone was important to me. Also, finding and talking with friends who did not know MJ. And talking about what I was feeling and going through also helped.

My experience was similar to Irene's. I needed friends who could understand that I needed to be alone. But I also needed new friends who knew me as an individual rather than as part of a couple, friends who were willing to listen to me talk about Emily. I felt that their understanding and support were critical to helping me link my previous life with Em to my current life without her.

Beverly had a friend who was unintentionally hurtful. In reflecting on what the friend had done, Beverly had a suggestion for what she could have done instead:

> The only person that I have not found helpful is one of our straight acquaintances who keeps inviting me to do things or to go on trips. She may be trying to be helpful, but those who know me best know to just let me know they are there, whenever I feel like company. That way, I do not feel pressured to do things that I really do not want to do.

The bottom line is to give your friend or family member the respect due her as a widow. If you will allow your widowed friend to talk about her deceased partner openly, no matter how much time has gone by, you will be helping her to heal. If she feels that she cannot talk openly with you, either about her deceased partner or how she feels about her partner's death, she may begin to avoid you because it is too painful to be with someone who cannot acknowledge her grief.

Another factor to take into consideration is whether or not your family member is out. If she is out and her loss can openly be acknowledged in all aspects of her life, she is more likely to be able to do the grief work she needs to do than a lesbian who is not out or who is only out in parts of her life. Either way, though, she needs you to listen to her.

GET THE HELP YOU NEED

This book has been written for lesbians who have been widowed, and this chapter offers advice to the friends and family who want to be supportive to them. However, in her study of bereaved lesbians in Ohio, Sharon Deevy (2000) made the point that it is not only the widow who suffers a loss. Friends and family members also grieve. I know that when Emily died, I may have been widowed, but a whole community of women had lost a friend. I was not able to reach out to them because I was too overwhelmed with my own grief. Likewise in this book, my focus has been on the experience of being widowed, not on the grief issues of lesbian friends. But I want to end this chapter by acknowledging the pain of friends and family members. I encourage you to find the support that you need too, just as you are trying to give support to your widowed friend or family member.

Chapter 15

For Professionals

In this chapter I look at three broad issues that need to be understood by professionals working with lesbian widows. One is grief and grief counseling. A second is the diversity within the lesbian community, and the third is the need for more support services directed specifically to lesbians.

GRIEF MODELS

While I was writing this book, I had occasion to visit my friend Juanita. It was September, and we were both feeling down as October, the month in which we were both widowed, was before us. We talked about how the time of year around our partner's death was still emotionally difficult for us. Yet friends who had never been widowed had a hard time understanding why, years later, we were still struggling.

In addition, I expressed my frustration with a phenomenon I had noticed with my graduate students. When they chose the topic of grief and presented reports on grief counseling or grief support groups in class, they inevitably introduced Kübler-Ross's five-stage model (Walter, 2003). Each time this happened, I would comment that her model was intended to express the stages people go through when they find out they are dying, and that there are other models of grief for those who have lost a loved one. I wondered why this seemed to be the only information on grief they researched. It is not an adequate model to describe our grief recovery experience as widows.

In response to my frustration, Juanita said, "Why don't you write that in your book?" Of course! So here it is: Using only Kübler-Ross's five stages of grief to counsel a widow is not very helpful. Something more is needed. I know that trained hospice volunteers and grief counselors understand this, but novice counseling professionals do not.

This five-stage model names only a few of the emotions that a widow experiences. The whole concept of stages is also problematic since grief does not happen in an orderly fashion. In addition, dealing with our emotions is only one part of our grief recovery, the stage we call grief work. We must also get to a place where we find life without our loved one meaningful again and create a whole new life without her.

Another misunderstanding about grief among novice counselors is that counselors can help clients get over their loss. The truth is that a widow will never get over her loss; she will never forget about or let go of her loved one. From a postmodern perspective on grief, we do not let go of our loved one but rather transform the relationship (Walter, 2003). What a counselor can do is assist the widow in learning to live with her grief in a less painful way and empower her to create a new sense of identity for herself without the partner.

There are many different models of grief counseling (Walter, 2003), but personally I identify most with a combination of a postmodern perspective and the concept of tasks that we need to accomplish rather than stages that we need to go through. This puts an emphasis on things that we can do to heal rather than thinking we can passively sit back and let time heal all wounds. Worden (2002) named four specific tasks: To accept the reality of the loss, to work through the pain of grief, to adjust to an environment in which the deceased is missing, and to emotionally relocate the deceased and move on with life.

When we counsel lesbian widows, we move into that area of grief work that involves addressing disenfranchised grief, grief that is not acknowledged by others. It is important for professionals to acknowledge that the loss of a partner by a lesbian is the same kind of traumatic loss as that of the married woman who loses her husband. It is not just the loss of a friend. At this time in history, when lesbians do not have the right to legally marry, it is critical that professionals accept and support lesbians who are widowed.

THE LESBIAN COMMUNITY

Although there are some commonalities between lesbian and married widows, lesbians face unique challenges. The relationship between two women is generally more intense than that between a man and a woman or between two men, and homophobia and heterosexism in society tend to draw lesbians even closer together (Ossana, 2000). In addition, widowed lesbians encounter hassles with the legal system since their relationship is not recognized as a legal marriage (Walter, 2003). All of these issues need to be considered in doing grief counseling with this population.

Another major difference between married and lesbian widows is to whom they turn for support. Typically, the married widow turns to her family. Typically the lesbian widow will turn to her chosen family, her extended friendship network in the lesbian community (Walter, 2003). Many of the lesbians included in this book did not look for support outside of their friends. Those who did had difficulty finding support services. A few felt disenfranchised by both the heterosexist culture and their lesbian community.

In working with a lesbian after her partner's death, counselors must take into consideration whether or not the lesbian is out and to whom, and whether or not she wants to come out to others during this time of mourning. This means understanding the coming-out process (Ritter and Terndrup, 2002). I am not sure that heterosexuals fully grasp what nonheterosexuals face in this culture; I know I did not fully appreciate the issue prior to my coming out in midlife. Although it may seem simple to think, "If she would just come out to others, she would get more support," that is not necessarily true. Even though I was pretty confident that I could have come out to my siblings and my colleagues at work when Emily was dying, I just did not have the emotional energy to take the risk. That is what it felt like to me, a risk. Caretaking and grieving left me too emotionally drained to take on any other hurdles, and I relied on the support of my friends, both lesbian and straight, who knew about my relationship with Em, and the therapist with whom I was working. I also had the additional weight of needing to honor Emily's privacy and not out her or our relationship to professionals working with her. After her death, when I moved to a new community, I was finally able to come out to others and receive additional support.

It is difficult for lesbians to believe that families who have not been accepting of their sexual orientation in the past might be supportive of them as widows. There are, of course, those who find otherwise. Ellen experienced a change of heart from her parents (Chapter 9) and

Walter (2003) reported that some lesbians she studied were also surprised to receive unexpected support. Anita (Chapter 5), however,
knew that support from her family would be limited; she could not
talk openly with them about her grief. Just as the grief process is
unique to each individual, it is important that professionals listen sen-
sitively to a lesbian widow's issues about whom she is willing to ask
for support and then respect her choice.

As with married widows, counselors can empower lesbian widows
to create new meaning in their lives and develop rituals of remembrance to make a place for the deceased partner in that new life. Dealing with legal and financial hassles due to their legally unrecognized
relationship adds another layer of loss to the lesbian widow's grief
process. Counselors can lend emotional support and provide information about local resources. If they believe that activism is part of
their professional responsibility, counselors can advocate for gay
marriage so that lesbian widows are afforded the same legal and
financial rights as married widows.

In addition to understanding the issue of whether or not the widow
is out and whether or not she wants to come out, professionals need to
appreciate that the lesbian community itself is quite diverse. No two
lesbian widows will be exactly alike. Sharon Deevey (2000), in her
research on bereavement experiences of lesbians in Ohio, emphasized this point and identified four different lesbian communities.
Deevey's description of different types of lesbian communities may
help grief workers better understand the diversity among their lesbian
clientele.

One lesbian community was identified by Deevey as the Big Village. This group includes lesbians who are in the closet, who fit in
with society, hide their private lives, and have no interactions with
other lesbians. Marilyn and Cheryl (Chapter 4) lived this way for
thirty-one years, having no contact that whole time with the LGBT
community.

The second community that Deevey identified was the Rainbow
Village. Here lesbians and gays work in the Big Village but are connected to the lesbian or gay communities privately. Ellen (Chapter 5)
and I were both in the Big Village at work but were part of a lesbian
community outside of work. We both came out to the Big Village
after our lovers died.

The Womyn's Land, the third lesbian community identified by Deevey, is where women live separate from the Big Village for the most part and place great emphasis on being with women. "Here lesbian couples and a few lesbian communes practice gender separatism, with a celebration of women and rural life as the major values" (Deevey, 2000, p. 10). Lois and Joan are a good example of a lesbian couple with this lifestyle. Their life together was heavily invested in women's music and women's community. They turned to their women's community for support as Joan was dying and received it.

The fourth community identified by Deevey was Carnival Village. This group emphasizes a lifestyle that tends to make society at large as well as the women in other villages uncomfortable. Drag, gender bending, queer theory, metal, leather, and tattoos are found here, but no one in my study indicated to me that they identified with this community. Professionals working with the lesbian population must educate themselves about the particular experiences that clients have had within these varied lesbian groupings.

In this book, I have only addressed the needs of lesbian widows. Deevey (2003) pointed out that professionals often neglect to provide support services for friends and family who are affected by the death too. Helping the widow's lesbian friends deal with their own grief while at the same time educating them about how they can best care for the widow needs to be considered part of the professional support services offered. Even the most supportive family and friends do not necessarily understand the grief process or how to be supportive to widows. The women in this particular study were widowed at young ages. This meant that their peers were too young to have experienced the death of a life partner, and they therefore lacked the ability to understand what their friend was going through. Providing information for them or helping the lesbian widow ask for what she needs is important.

THE NEED FOR MORE RESOURCES

The lack of support groups for lesbian widows is an obvious problem, as is the lack of written literature available for this population. Creating grief support groups specifically for lesbians would be a positive step to take where possible. In the absence of the ability to provide this service, counselors can assist widows with creating support networks for themselves.

The widows in this book who hurt the most, even years after their partner's death, were those lesbians who did not receive support from their lesbian friends or who could not find a lesbian bereavement group at their local lesbian health or cancer center. Thus, the charge in this book is not just to grief specialists but to lesbian health specialists who ignore the needs of lesbian widows. Lesbians who were not well-connected to the local lesbian community faced the most severe lack of support, suffering in isolation, the worst way to face the grief recovery process. But those who thought they were well-connected to their lesbian community and still did not receive support felt bitter even years later.

Working with lesbian widows requires understanding of two broad areas of expertise for professionals. First is an understanding of grief itself. Second is an understanding of lesbian relationships and friendship networks. Underlying those areas of expertise must be the acceptance of the validity of lesbian relationships and the recognition that the surviving partner is indeed a widow. In response to this book, I hope that the professional community will recognize its responsibility to end the invisibility of lesbians by creating more support services and written materials specifically for lesbians.

Appendix A

The Lesbian Widows

Five widows gave permission to use their real names, indicated below by an asterisk (*) after their names. For the remainder I have changed not only their names but also identifying information, such as where they lived, in order to maintain the confidentiality I guaranteed to them.

Janet and Chris

Janet was widowed at age thirty. She and Chris met in an emergency room when Janet was a paramedic with the fire department and Chris was a police officer with the highway patrol; they were both in their early twenties. They had eight years together before Chris was shot and killed at work. It has been seventeen years since Chris's death, and Janet is now a personal coach and life trainer, helping others who have lost a loved one.

*Beverly and Virginia**

Beverly York met Virginia through a friend when she was twenty-six and Virginia was thirty-two. Virginia beat one bout of cancer in the early 1990s, but the cancer returned seven years later. Beverly was her only caretaker during her illness. When Virginia passed away, they had been together for almost thirty-seven years.

Cassie and Fran

As soon as they met each other, Cassie and Fran knew instantly that they were soul mates and wanted to spend the rest of their lives together. Cassie fondly called Fran her Tex-Mex. They loved each other for only nine months before Fran died unexpectedly one night of heart failure.

*Irene and MJ**

Irene Schreiber and MJ met playing on the same softball team when they were twenty-eight and thirty-one respectively. After nine months, they moved in together, and friends told them they were role models of the ideal couple. They had been together twenty years when MJ died from breast cancer.

Dale and Carol

Dale was thirty-five and a graduate student when she met Carol, age forty-six and a university professor. Dale went through a difficult divorce, careful to hide her relationship with Carol so she would not lose custody of her three children. Carol had been diagnosed with MS prior to their meeting but was in relatively good health when Carol's divorce was final and they bought a house together. Then Carol's health began to deteriorate. Eventually Dale had to move Carol to a nursing home, where she stayed for seven years until the day she died in Dale's arms. They were together a total of fourteen years.

Linda and Tonya

Linda and her partner became friends with Tonya and her partner. Even though they lived in different states, they enjoyed the rare times they were able to spend together. Linda and Tonya supported each other by telephone through their breakups with their partners and later they moved in together. Tonya underwent gastric bypass surgery and had one complication after another, dying four months later. They had been together for only two and a half years. Linda was forty-four years old when Tonya died; Tonya was only thirty-eight.

Maureen and Robin

Maureen and Robin met when working in the same hospital, Maureen as a rehabilitation therapist and Robin as a nurse. Robin was twenty years older than Maureen and had three grown children, but she agreed to support Maureen in becoming pregnant and raising a child. Robin had been successfully treated for breast cancer five years before they partnered, but the cancer recurred and Robin died when Maureen was six months pregnant. The loss was devastating to Maureen; she was thirty-four years old.

Anna Marie and Caroline

Anna Marie described her relationship with Caroline as rocky in the beginning. Caroline was recently divorced and had two children who sometimes lived with them, sometimes with their father. Shortly after they moved in together, Caroline began having stomachaches that eventually became so severe that Anna Marie had to rush her to the emergency room. Stomach cancer. That was the beginning of many trips to the emergency room. Caroline passed away surrounded by family and friends who loved her. Anna Marie and Caroline had been together for seven years, leaving Anna Marie a widow at age forty-three.

Donna and Randi

Donna met Randi when Randi's daughter-in-law, who sang in a chorus with Donna, introduced them. They felt instantly that they were soul mates, and eventually they purchased a home together. According to Donna, friends and family saw their relationship as joyous. After four years together, Randi was diagnosed with lung cancer. She lived another three years, leaving Donna a widow at age forty-nine.

Joy and Barbara*

Joy Griffith met Barbara at a Golden Threads Celebration in Provincetown when she was fifty-three and Barbara was fifty-six. Joy was teaching in Germany; Barbara had been born in London but was living in New Zealand. Barbara temporarily returned to New Zealand to close down her home and then went to Germany to be with Joy. After a couple of years together, Barbara became sick with what she told Joy was pneumonia. Barbara reported that her doctor advised that she return to the warmer climate of New Zealand. Once there, she told Joy by telephone that she actually had inoperable lung cancer. She died in New Zealand, not wanting to burden Joy with her care.

Samantha and Marie

A lesbian bar was the meeting place for Samantha and Marie. Marie had recently moved to the United States from South America. Samantha was a firefighter and Marie a graduate student working on a PhD. They fought a lot, and fought passionately, but they loved passionately too. After five years together, Marie was diagnosed with advanced breast cancer. After treatment, the cancer spread to her brain. She died on Christmas Day, forever making that holiday difficult for Samantha. Samantha was forty-two and Marie was only thirty-four when she died.

Lois and Joan*

Lois Reborne and Joan Driskell met when Lois was twenty-nine and Joan was twenty-six. They worked together for thirteen years in a home remodeling business. They were also organizers of the Midwest Women's Festival for many years. Another group important to them for twelve of the years they were together was the Kansas City Women's Chorus. Joan was diagnosed with ovarian cancer, which later spread to her lungs. As she was caring for Joan, Lois said that she fell in love with her all over again. They had nineteen years together before Joan passed away.

Rose and Steph

Rose got to know Steph when they worked in administrative positions in the same hospital; she was married at the time and Steph was an out lesbian. Eventually Rose divorced and Steph moved in with her. Steph had a history of heart problems and ended up having to quit her job and live on disability. It was a turbulent relationship, and eventually they broke up. Even though Steph moved to another state, they maintained contact with each other and talked on the phone for hours every day, having a sense of soul connection. Steph died of complications of her heart condition after emergency surgery on Christmas Day.

Shirley and Terry*

After two divorces, four children, and four stepchildren, Shirley Hansen fell in love with Terry, her first female lover. Terry operated a day care center in the home they shared, and Shirley worked as a social worker in a nursing home. Eleven years later, Terry died unexpectedly of a massive heart attack. Shirley remembers being angry with Terry for leaving her and not taking care of herself. Shirley was fifty-four and Terry was thirty-eight when she died.

Marilyn and Cheryl

Marilyn met Cheryl when she was twenty-one and Cheryl was twenty-six years old. Marilyn's admiration for Cheryl's work with the handicapped led to friendship and then love. They purchased a home together, adopted and raised three children with disabilities, and had thirty-one loving years together, centering their lives on their children. Their life together was shattered when Cheryl was diagnosed with and then died of bulbar-onset ALS. They had lived in the closet for those thirty-one years, but Marilyn came out when Cheryl died.

Pat and Betty

Betty, age twenty-two, and Pat, twenty, met on a WAC softball team when they were both stationed in the army. This was pre-Stonewall, and being out was not an option. Eventually they both left the army, went back to school, and moved together to various work locations over the years. Sixteen years into their relationship, Betty was diagnosed with breast cancer and had a radical mastectomy. Thirteen years after that, she was diagnosed with cancer in the duodenum and liver, and she was given only months to live. Betty fought and lived for another year, dying after they had spent a total of thirty-two years together.

Nora and Anne

Anne and Nora were close friends for about two years and lovers for about five months before Anne passed away from lung cancer. Friends warned Nora not to get involved since Anne already had lung cancer, but Nora wanted to believe that love could work miracles. Nora wrote, "Although we knew there could not be a far distant future, we talked about the life we could have together." Anne's death was a double tragedy for Nora; her oldest son had died the previous year. She was forty-seven years old when Anne died.

Pam and Sandy

When Pam met Sandy, she was intrigued by the realization that she was not the only Jewish lesbian in the world. When they became lovers three years later, Pam was thirty and Sandy was forty-eight. They had a commitment ceremony one year later. Sandy's mother had died of breast cancer when Sandy was only sixteen; Sandy herself was diagnosed with breast cancer for the first time at age forty. Later she had cancerous lumps in her lungs removed. Sandy died ten years after they began their life together, leaving Pam a widow at age forty.

Ellen and Kate

Ellen was in the process of divorcing her husband of seventeen years when she met Kate at a healing group for a mutual friend. Their spiritual connection remained strong throughout their relationship. When they moved in together, after Ellen's divorce was final, Kate coparented Ellen's two children. Tragically, after six years together, Kate was killed in a car accident while they were on vacation. Ellen was forty-two when she was widowed.

Traci and Dana

According to Traci, she and Dana, having been lesbians for many years prior to meeting each other, knew what they wanted, and they knew this was it. They were part of a large community of lesbian friends who told them that they were role models to the rest of them. Sixteen years later, however, Dana discovered a lump on her neck that turned out to be lung cancer. They were eating dinner one night when Dana stopped breathing. Traci and Dana were both forty-six when Dana died.

Jane and Lynn

Jane and Lynn shared a passion for dance and formed a small dance company together. Jane was twenty-one and Lynn was twenty-eight when they became lovers; a year later they had a formal commitment ceremony. For twenty-three years they lived and worked together. Lynn was treated for breast cancer and survived five years, but then she began to have mood swings and a cough; the cancer had returned. Though she made a valiant effort to survive, Lynn passed away before another round of chemotherapy could begin. Jane was forty-four years old at the time.

Vera and Nancy

Nancy and Vera met when Nancy was being kicked out of a relationship and Vera was ending her marriage of fifteen years. Nancy was determined not to get into another relationship too soon, whereas Vera was immediately ready to settle down. It was a rocky first year but they hung in there. Ten years into the relationship, Nancy had surgery and treatment for ovarian cancer; she felt better for a couple of years before the cancer returned. Vera did not realize Nancy was dying until just before the end. They had been together for sixteen years. Vera was forty-five and Nancy was fifty-four when Nancy passed away.

Heather and Ruth

Heather was the youngest widow in this book, age twenty-nine. She and Ruth met working on a lesbian hotline when Heather was in college and Ruth was on disability due to diabetes. Ruth's friends disapproved of this "baby dyke," fearing she would break Ruth's heart, but they were truly in love. There were many medical crises over the seven years they were together. One day Ruth took a nap and never woke up.

Anita and Holly

Anita and Holly had a commuter relationship for eight years. Holly lived with her elderly and disabled mother and Anita taught college two hours away. They spent holidays and vacations together and loved to travel. After Holly's mother died, however, Holly began drinking heavily. She died suddenly and unexpectedly one day of a massive cerebral hemorrhage. Anita was widowed at age sixty-six.

Appendix B

Resources

The following are the books that the widows in *Lesbian Widows: Invisible Grief* found helpful in the absence of any grief book written specifically for lesbians. It is not intended to be a comprehensive list of everything available on grief, nor is it an endorsement of any particular book.

Bolen, J. S. (1998). *Close to the bone: Life-threatening illness and the search for meaning.* New York: Touchstone.

Bono, C. (with Kort, M.). (2002). *The end of innocence: A memoir.* Los Angeles: Advocate Books.

Butler, S. and Rosenblum, B. (1991). *Cancer in two voices* (Expanded ed.). Duluth, MN: Spinsters Ink.

Davidson, J. D. and Doka, K. J. (Eds.). (1999). *Living with grief at work, at school, at worship.* Washington, DC: Hospice Foundation of America.

Hickman, M. W. (1994). *Healing after loss: Daily meditations for working through grief.* New York: Avon Books, Inc.

Kusher, H. (1981). *When bad things happen to good people.* New York: Avon Books, Inc.

Lewis, C. S. (1961). *A grief observed.* New York: HarperCollins Publishers.

Neeld, E. H. (2003). *Seven choices: Finding daylight after loss shatters your world.* Austin, TX: Centerpoint Press.

Pace, A. L. (1996). *Write from the heart: Lesbians healing from heartache.* Beaverton, OR: Baby Steps Press.

Rapoport, N. (1994). *A woman's book of grieving.* New York: William Morrow and Company, Inc.

Staudacher, C. (1994). *A time to grieve: Meditations for healing after the death of a loved one.* New York: HarperCollins Publishers.

Stern, E. S. (1995). *Living with loss (Days of healing, days of change).* New York: Dell Publishing Co.

Note: One person mentioned "Living with Grief" by Davidson and Doka and I had to guess what book she meant because there are two books by these authors that start with "Living with Grief." I have listed *Living with Grief at Work, at School, at Worship* here because she listed Davidson as the first author whereas *Living with Grief: Who We Are, How We Grieve* lists Doka first (and this book is listed in the Bibliography).

Bibliography

Becvar, D. S. (2001). *In the presence of grief: Helping family members resolve death, dying, and bereavement issues.* New York: The Guilford Press.

Bono, C. (with Kort, M.). (2002). *The end of innocence: A memoir.* Los Angeles: Advocate Books.

Butler, S. and Rosenblum, B. (1991). *Cancer in two voices.* Duluth, MN: Spinsters Ink.

Davidson, J. D. and Doka, K. J. (Eds.). (1999). *Living with grief at work, at school, at worship.* Washington, DC: Hospice Foundation of America.

Deevey, S. (2000). Cultural variation in lesbian bereavement experiences. *Journal of the Gay and Lesbian Medical Association, 4*(1), 9-17.

Doka, K. J. (Ed.). (2002). *Disenfranchised grief: New directions, challenges, and strategies for practice.* Champaign, IL: Research Press.

Doka, K. J. and Davidson, J. D. (Eds.). (1998). *Living with grief: Who we are, how we grieve.* Washington, DC: Hospice Foundation of America.

Fitzgerald, H. (1994). *The mourning handbook.* New York: Fireside.

James, J. W. and Friedman, R. (1998). *The grief recovery handbook: The action program for moving beyond death, divorce, and other losses.* New York: Harper/Perennial.

O'Neill, C. and Ritter, K. (1992). *Coming out within: Stages of spiritual awakening for lesbians and gay men.* New York: Harper San Francisco.

Ossana, S. M. (2000). *Relationship and couples counseling.* In Perez, R. M., DeBord, K. A., and Bieschke, K. J. (Eds.). *Handbook of counseling and psychotherapy with lesbian, gay, and bisexual clients* (pp. 275-302). Washington, DC: American Psychological Association.

Perez, R. M., DeBord, K. A., and Bieschke, K. J. (Eds.). (2000). *Handbook of counseling and psychotherapy with lesbian, gay, and bisexual clients.* Washington, DC: American Psychological Association.

Rando, T. A. (1988). *Grieving: How to go on living when someone you love dies.* New York: Lexington Books.

Ritter, K. Y. and Terndrup, A. I. (2002). *Handbook of affirmative psychotherapy with lesbians and gay men.* New York: The Guilford Press.

Seidman, I. E. (1991). *Interviewing as qualitative research: A guide for researchers in education and the social sciences.* New York: Teachers College Press.

Walter, C. A. (2003). *The loss of a life partner: Narratives of the bereaved.* New York: Columbia University Press.

Wilder, R. E. (1998). Sexual orientation and grief. In Doka, K. J. and Davidson, J. D. *Living with grief: Who we are, how we grieve* (pp. 199-206). Washington, DC: Hospice Foundation of America.

Wolfelt, A. D. (1992). *Understanding grief: Helping yourself heal.* Levittown, PA: Accelerated Development.

Worden, J. W. (2002). *Grief counseling and grief therapy* (3rd ed.). New York: Springer.

Index